FIRESIDE

PARKSIDE

FIRESIDE ✦ PARKSIDE BOOKS

Addictionary: A Primer of Recovery Terms from Abstinence to Withdrawal, by Jan R. Wilson, C.E.D.C., C.A.P., and Judith A. Wilson, C.A.P.

Anatomy of a Food Addiction: The Brain Chemistry of Overeating, by Anne Katherine, M.A.

Behind the 8-Ball: A Guide for Families of Gamblers, by Linda Berman, M.S.W., and Mary-Ellen Siegel, M.S.W.

Believing in Myself: Daily Meditations for Healing and Building Self-Esteem, by Earnie Larsen and Carol Hegarty

Blues Ain't Nothing But a Good Soul Feeling Bad: Daily Steps to Spiritual Growth, by Sheldon Kopp with Bonnie B. Hesse

Codependents' Guide to the Twelve Steps, by Melody Beattie

Compassionate Touch: The Role of Human Touch in Healing and Recovery, by Clyde Ford

Freedom from Food: The Secret Lives of Dieters and Compulsive Eaters, by Elizabeth Hampshire

From Love That Hurts to Love That's Real: A Recovery Workbook, by Sylvia Ogden Peterson

Growing Through the Pain: The Incest Survivor's Companion, by Catherine Bronson

Growing Up Gay in a Dysfunctional Family: A Guide for Gay Men Reclaiming Their Lives, by Rik Isensee

Help for Helpers: Daily Meditations for Those Who Care

MEDITATIONS

FOR PARENTS

Who Do

TOO MUCH

Jonathon and Wendy Lazear

A Fireside/Parkside Meditation Book
Published by Simon & Schuster
New York London Toronto Sydney Tokyo Singapore

FIRESIDE/PARKSIDE

Rockfeller Center
1230 Avenue of the Americas
New York, New York 10020

Designed by Bonni Leon-Berman
Manufactured in the United States of America

3 5 7 9 10 8 6 4

Library of Congress Cataloging-in-Publication Data is available.

ISBN: 0-671-79635-6

Parkside Medical Services Corporation is a full-service
provider of treatment for alcoholism, other drug addiction,
eating disorders, and psychiatric illness.

Parkside Medical Services Corporation
205 West Touhy Avenue
Park Ridge, IL 60058
1-800-PARKSIDE

To Our Parents,
Jon, Virginia, George, and Alice
And Our Children,
Michael and Ross

ACKNOWLEDGMENTS

We wish to thank our children, Michael and Ross, as our primary teachers in the laboratory of parenthood, for their wisdom and their humor. Thanks to our parents, Jon and Virginia Lazear and Alice and George Broad, from whom we learned so much.

We thank the following people who helped make this book a reality: Anne Wilson Schaef for her courage, insight, and friendship; Diane Fassel for her kindness and intelligence; Melody Beattie for her extraordinary inspiration and strength; Marilyn Abraham, our editorial leader and friend; Sheila Curry, our editor; John Small of Parkside Publishing; Carol Hegarty, a virtual fountain of ideas, all of them good; Gary Paulsen, whose kindness and humanity has touched us directly, and millions of others through his books; Earnie Larsen, who inspires so many to be all that they can be; Harold Bloomfield and Sirah Vettese, who know how to live from their hearts; Alan Loy McGinnis for his fine work; Ellen Sue Stern, who has generously created a veritable library of good works in the field of wellness and recovery; Phillip Berman, who is a new friend and brilliant theologian; Tom Grady and Clayton Carlson, friends with great minds; Pat Carnes, the father of a very important component of recovery; Wayne Kritsberg, a gentle but guiding force in the world of the wellness movement; Robert Cooper, who is prolific as he is creative; Natalie Goldberg for being Natalie Goldberg.

A warm thank you to the Friedberg family, and appreciation to our staff workers, Bonnie Blodgett, Susie Moncur, Eric Vrooman, and Dennis Cass; also to Jennifer Flannery.

And finally, to exceptional parents we know and admire: Tony and Nina Borwick, Lynn and Conni Guyer, Tim and Rosemary Rumsey, Gene and Gay Kassan, Will and Rose Weaver, George and Kate Cleveland, Beverly Wilson, Doug and Paula Super, Paul and Teddy Stang, Harvey and Carol Ann Mackay, Brian and Ruth Nowak, Brian and Pam Henjum, Jon and Debra Orenstein, Cam and Bonnie Blodgett, Drew and Ellen Stewart, Terry Spohn, Leona Nevler, Jim Silberman, Phil and Estelle Schneider, Howard and Judy Seed, Gertrude and Harry Bergen, Joe and Sylvie Hess, Karen and Nick Morrison, Gail and Hank See, Bill and Mary Wells, Gale and Sherry Knappenberger, Tom and Dottie Dekko, Jack and Mary Willis, Dale Burg and Dick Nusser.

MEDITATIONS

FOR PARENTS

Who do

TOO MUCH

If a child is to keep alive his inborn sense of wonder, he needs the companionship of at least one adult who can share it, rediscovering with him the joy, excitement and mystery of the world we live in.

—*Rachel Carson*

Parents who do too much may try to do more for their children than there are hours in the day. As a result, we end up depleted and frustrated and may feel as if we have failed. The day begins with lists and wishes. It ends with more lists and unfulfilled wishes.

Our children need us as more than just "doers." If all we do is drive them to lessons, prepare them the healthiest snacks, buy them the latest toys, we are missing the point.

What our children need from us is our companionship. If we forget this we will lose more than just hours in a day.

◆

I will try to take time out today to rediscover what it is to be a child. If I restore my sense of wonder, I may replenish my spirit and give my child a great gift.

Parenthood remains the greatest single preserve of the amateur.

—*Alvin Toffler*

There are no requirements for this job. We don't need to pass a test or know someone at the top. We're parents because we want to be parents. That's the only requirement.

Once we have the job we realize that we are unprepared for it and we are forced to learn how to do it by doing it. Experience is our teacher. We get through the days and weeks and months by simply doing the best we can, all the while, doubting that we are equal to the task.

It helps to remember that we are not alone. If we seem to be on overload as parents—in over our heads—we should remember that others before and since, including our own parents, felt the same way.

◆

I will remember, that like the parents who came before me and the ones who will come after, I am an amateur and every day is a learning process.

The first duty of love is to listen.

—*Paul Tillich*

Parents who do too much tend not to spend enough time listening to their children. Instead, time is engaged in all those "active" pursuits—driving, shopping, talking, lecturing.

But listening is not just our right as parents—it is our "duty." We owe it to our children, as we owe it to ourselves, to hear what they have to say to us. And if we are too busy endlessly arranging their lives, we run the risk of being great managers and lousy parents.

One reason we don't listen to our children enough, is that children don't really know how to ask us to listen. Sometimes they shout or make demands, and we tune them out. We need to recognize a need that often goes unspoken. We need to respond even when there is no call.

◆

Today I will tune out all the extraneous attention seekers in my environment—the telephone, the television, the work—and make time for listening.

January 4

You know more than you think you do.

—*Benjamin Spock*

If we could only hear ourselves think. We do hear the latest talk-show expert—we remember what he or she said and try to apply it to our lives. But our own thoughts are muffled by a constant barrage of media, well-meaning friends and relatives, and the challenges that come from our children themselves.

We need to trust our instincts. We may be amateurs in this parenting business, but one ounce of instinct is worth a pound of advice.

In our society it is increasingly hard to screen out the external experts. But we will find that the more we follow our instincts, the more we get used to hearing our own voice above the others, the more control we will have over our lives.

◆

I must find some time today to listen to the sound of my inner voice.

Any parent who has ever found a rusted toy automobile buried in the grass or a bent sandbucket on the beach knows that objects like these can be among the most powerful things in the world.

—*Sports Illustrated*

There are days when we feel lost. There is so much to accomplish, and so little time. We fear that we are missing out on the fun—that our children are growing up and we barely have time to notice.

Someday, we will look through boxes of old toys, rummaging for memories. This does not mean, however, that we should fail to notice what is ours here and now.

Although we are building a wonderful memory bank, we mustn't rely on it. Now and then, we must embrace our role as parents, forsaking our sense of commitment for our sense of joy.

◆

I want to be a participant in my children's growth, not a bystander. I will take the time to appreciate the here and now.

My mother had a great deal of trouble with me, but I think she enjoyed it.

—*Mark Twain*

Sometimes to "do too much" means we are doing too much for our kids. Thinking about them, worrying about them, suffering for them. If our kids think we "enjoy" this kind of involvement, they may allow us to feed on their problems, and thereby avoid handling situations for themselves.

Obviously, this is disastrous. Our kids are hooked on what they perceive as our need to run their lives. And we are hooked on the notion that they cannot handle things for themselves.

This is codependent behavior of the worst kind. Our kids need to learn to suffer the consequences of their own choices—good or bad. And we need to learn to let them. In this case, "doing too much" is far more damaging than doing nothing at all.

◆

I will enjoy watching my children today, appreciating their innate ability to find solutions to life's problems. I will respond if help is needed, but otherwise I will find enjoyment in quiet observation.

Ask your child what he wants for dinner only if he is buying.

—*Fran Lebowitz*

How many times have we bent over backward to please our children, gone the extra mile—only to find ourselves completely overwhelmed?

If, at the end of a long day filled with responsibilities of all kinds, we don't have time to satisfy our children's whims—we can forgive ourselves. It is okay for our children to hear the words "no," and "not now."

We are making the very best of our lives if all we do is try. Our children will understand this—and accept it.

◆

Today I will remind myself that I cannot please everyone every time. I will please my children more by not offering them what I do not always have to give.

There are only two lasting bequests we can hope to give our children. One of these is roots. The other, wings.

—*Hodding Carter*

We often tell ourselves that what we do—our busy schedules, our full calendars, our extra work loads—we do for our children. But all we can really hope to give our children is the freedom to live their own lives.

Yes, we can provide for them. We can put bread on the table and books on the shelves. We can even lend them our wisdom and tell them of our past. But we cannot design their future, and they would not want us to.

The real challenge of parenting is to do just enough—and no more.

◆

I will reflect upon my own roots and think about the first time I left home. I will remember that my children will some day have lives of their own.

To bring up a child in the way he should go, travel that way yourself once in a while.

—*Josh Billings*

If we are stuck in a dead-end job or one which gives us little satisfaction; if we have no time to explore other options; then what are we teaching our children? Are we teaching them to give up their ideals, their dreams, too? Are we showing them that there are no choices in life, only compromises?

We must remember that our children learn by our example. They may not always hear what we say, but they almost always watch what we do.

◆

I will take some time to think about my own needs. I will make a list of promises to myself that I will try my best to keep.

He who laughs, lasts.

—*Anonymous*

We need to be reminded of the power of laughter. No matter how much we need to get done, it is better to sacrifice some of our work time than to sacrifice our sense of humor.

We must remember that we are parents, not robocops. We cannot simply put ourselves on automatic pilot and walk through the day unscathed. Nor can we put on a suit of armor and prevent ourselves from getting hurt. Nothing can prepare us for the daily tasks we must face, the fences we must mend, the crises we must solve.

Nothing can prepare us—but one thing can offer us solace: our ability to laugh. As parents, we should never underestimate the importance of a good laugh at the end of a trying day.

◆

I will try to find time today to laugh with my children and my spouse. Have I really forgotten how to have fun?

Half our mistakes in life arise from feeling where we ought to think, and thinking where we ought to feel.
—*J. Churton Collins*

As parents who "do too much" we are often parents who "think too much." Mistrusting our instincts, misreading our inner cues, we make the mistake of letting our thoughts dictate.

When we are dealing with our children, we may not always "think" of the right answer, but if we try to "feel" our way along, the answer may come to us.

◆

Today I will make a decision that is based solely on the way I "feel." I will enjoy the comfort that this kind of decision-making brings.

The best is the enemy of the good.

—Voltaire

In our society we are always striving to be "the best." We tell our children to be "the very best" they can be. We push ourselves, as the saying goes, "to the max."

But there is danger in this behavior. Pushing ourselves, driving ourselves to be "the best" runs the risk of great loss: loss of time with our children, loss of leisure, loss of health. We can be "good enough" parents, employees, spouses. We can be "good enough" human beings.

We must learn to have some sense of satisfaction in the small things we accomplish—and understand that "the best," "the most," "the greatest," may be an unrealistic goal—for ourselves and our children.

◆

I need to recognize the potential destructiveness of my perfectionism.

I have a new philosophy. I'm only going to dread
one day at a time.

—*Charles M. Schulz*

When you're on a treadmill, every day seems insurmountable. There are "promises to keep," and "miles
to go before you sleep."

It is important to keep things in perspective. Try not
to see the mountains that are just beyond the hills.
Take it one step at a time, one day at a time. We need
to see parenting in the same way we see our other
"jobs": we are learning every day, striving toward a distant goal. We do *have* a goal: raising healthy, productive children. The goal will be realized. Some day our
children will become independent.

◆

*I will concentrate on what I must get done today and not be
overwhelmed by what I may have to do tomorrow.*

We know what happens to people who stay in the middle of the road. They get run over.

—*Aneurin Bevan*

One of the biggest stumbling blocks we face as parents is the challenge of commitment. Some days just making a decision, without consulting our neighbors, friends, or latest parenting "manual," seems impossible. Busy lives interfere with our ability to think—and often we give our children answers, only to find ourselves wondering, minutes later, if they are the right ones.

But commitment is important. Our children need to know where we stand. It's okay to change your mind—but it's not okay to second-guess every thought, decision, or rule.

◆

Today I will try to focus on any issues that arise. I will put off making important decisions rather than give hasty answers.

As a child, my family's menu consisted of two choices: take it or leave it.

—*Buddy Hackett*

Maybe we give our kids too much latitude. We hear about the old days, when kids didn't have so much freedom of choice. We hear that too much permissiveness, too few limits are harmful.

Yet we're part of a generation that believes in freedom. We ask our kids what they want for dinner instead of just putting dinner on the table. We tell them what we expect from them instead of asking them what they expect from us.

If we are to find peace, we need to strike a balance. Certainly our kids need to have some say in their own lives. But if we turn over the baton too eagerly, we may find ourselves playing whatever song they want us to play, whenever they want us to play it.

◆

I will try to give my children choices today and will be comfortable with whatever they choose.

All my children have spoken for themselves since they first learned to speak, and not always with my advance approval, and I expect that to continue in the future.

—*Gerald Ford*

If we are exhausted parents, it may be because we are too controlling. If we find ourselves hanging on our child's every word, planning his future, choosing his friends, and fighting his enemies, it may be that we need to take a giant step backward.

Our kids need to ask our permission, but then they need to act on their own. We cannot always be there to speak for them. We should not. Without our voices whispering in the background, our children's voices will have a chance to resonate.

Sometimes, doing too much can be destructive. We need to ask ourselves what we are doing for our children that they are fully capable of doing for themselves.

◆

Today I will think about all the decisions I have made for my children this past week. How many of those decisions could they have made for themselves?

As we read the school reports on our children, we realize a sense of relief that can rise to delight that—thank heaven—nobody is reporting in this fashion on us.

—*J. B. Priestley*

Parents don't get report cards. We muddle through, with little feedback of any kind, wondering if we're doing well or just passing.

The truth is, this job doesn't reward us—at least not in full measure—for many years. We may experience pleasure, amusement, joy. But we will not know, for many years, if we've been successful parents.

We should probably not feel too bad about this. Parenting may be one of the few things in life we can relax and enjoy—if we let ourselves. Nobody's grading us—except ourselves. And, really, just for effort, we should give ourselves high marks.

◆

I will try to stop "grading" myself as a parent. Instead, I will make an effort to relax and enjoy what I do.

All children alarm their parents, if only because you are forever expecting to encounter yourself.

—*Gore Vidal*

Remember the first time you heard your child say something that reminded you exactly of yourself? Did you feel proud? Or did you, like most of us, cringe just a little?

We may not be frightened by our kids until they begin to resemble us. Then, we are afraid of them, as if they were ghosts of our own childhood. And we are afraid for them, because we remember the pain of growing up.

We have to remind ourselves that our children are separate beings. They may have our noses, our eyes, our smiles, our tempers—but they are not us.

◆

I realize that my children are different from me, and that they will lead their own lives.

Schoolmasters and parents exist to be grown out of.
—*John Wolfenden*

Wanted: Caretaker, supervisor, to provide love, nurturing, financial and emotional security. If job is well done, in about eighteen years you will no longer be needed. Benefits include occasional hugs. No previous experience necessary.

What kind of a job is this, and why do we all apply for it? Is it for the feeling like no other that we get when our son or daughter puts those tiny arms around our necks, looks into our eyes, and says "I love you"?

If we are burned out as parents, it may not be the job—but the way we perceive the job—that is to blame.

◆

Being a parent has its frustrations, but it also has its rewards. I will think about how much joy I get from being a parent.

One of the advantages of being disorderly is that one is constantly making exciting discoveries.

—*A. A. Milne*

We hear lots of parents complain that they are so busy doing other things that they have little "quality" time for their kids.

But if we're going to find that time, we may have to relax our standards. We may have to let the laundry pile up, let a day's phone messages lapse, let the dog go without his bath. A little "disorder," may be necessary, if we're going to find the time to read that bedtime story.

When did "orderly" lives become so important? Why do we need to go to bed every night with every item crossed off our list?

◆

Today I will make a point of not getting everything done. I will use the "extra" time I've created to play with my children.

And my parents finally realize that I'm kidnapped and they snap into action immediately. They rent out my room.

—*Woody Allen*

We probably think our kids feel secure. They know we love them, and no matter how mad we get, we'd never trade them for another child. Right? Wrong. Most kids are insecure and need constant proof of our love.

But if we allow ourselves to feel guilty because we don't spend enough time with them, we are just filling up our already overloaded brains with one more negative thought.

We do what we can. Kids will probably always have these insecurities—no matter how much "quality time" we arrange. This may even be the way they are—subliminally—preparing themselves for the time they must leave us.

◆

I will not allow myself to feel guilty about spending too little time with my kids. I will look at the time I do spend as positive and meaningful.

Literature is mostly about having sex and not much about having children. Life is the other way around.
—*David Lodge*

Doing too much can mean too little time for pleasure—and most new parents will confirm that this is true.

It's strange, really, because you and your spouse have just produced—together—this beautiful new being—a living testament to your love. But suddenly you have no time for each other. Three is a magical number, but it's also "a crowd."

Remember what brought you to this moment and try to find the time—maybe not as much as you had before the baby was born—to be alone together.

◆

Today I will try to spend more time thinking about life's pleasures. I've neglected them for too long.

I praise casualness. It seems the rarest of virtues. It is useful enough when children are small. It is important to the point of necessity when they are adolescents.

—*Phyllis McGinley*

Stay calm. Don't panic. Be casual. If it's raining, find an umbrella. Sometimes it's the simplest thing that solves the problem. Don't always look for complex solutions.

Maybe we need to slow up a bit, play our lives on a different speed. There's a momentum that builds, daily, until we're breathless. The pace is too tough. And life seems out of control.

We must try to remember that we are the ones who control the pace. We can accomplish more by being casual, than by running ahead at full speed.

◆

I will try to have a casual morning and see how that affects the rest of my day.

I have found the best way to give advice to your children is to find out what they want and then advise them to do it.

—*Harry S. Truman*

We don't want to stand on a soap box, especially when we're talking to our teenagers.

Maybe Truman had the right idea. Administer to our children the advice they want to hear. They may respect us, and return for more advice. And pretty soon we have a good thing going. Kindness and respect. Isn't that what parenting should really be about?

If we are busy, so are our children. We need to respect and nurture their values if we want them to notice ours.

◆

I must try to be more of a sympathetic listener than an adviser. I want my children to feel that I support them.

Our children are not going to be just "our children"—they are going to be other people's husbands and wives and the parents of our grandchildren.

—*Mary S. Calderone*

It's important to remember this. Maybe we've learned not to smother our children. But do we really know and accept in our hearts that our children are individuals, separate from us?

When we do too much for our children, we are not just "spoiling" them, we are luring them into a trap. They become addicted to the things we do for them and resent us for it. There is no happy outcome here.

It is better to foster their independence and let them go. Then, we can be certain that they will return.

◆

I will spend some time imagining my children as grown men and women. I will also try to think about what role I'd like to play in their future lives.

To each other, we were as normal and nice as the smell of bread. We were just a family. In a family even exaggerations make perfect sense.

—*John Irving*

When you are exhausted after a day's work, you return to your family. What you seek is comfort—not more stress.

It is important that your home be a respite, a place where your energy is restored, not dissipated. The family nurtures you, warms you, readies you for another grueling day in the outside world.

Families break apart when they begin to seem more stressful than work. Perhaps we need to remind ourselves not to turn our home life into "work," or think of parenting as a "job."

◆

Tonight I will try to have fun with my children, putting aside the tensions of the day, and letting their pure and innocent joy welcome me home.

Example is not the main thing in influencing others.
It is the only thing.

—*Albert Schweitzer*

If your kids are beginning to sound like you, it is no accident. For no matter what you read to them, relate to them, show them on television, your kids are basically imitating no one else but you.

Children want to look up to their parents. And if they see parents who are tired all the time, running through life at breakneck speed, they will undoubtedly handle their schoolwork, if not their life's work, in a similar way.

If we are worried about the way our kids are behaving, maybe we ought to take a look at the state of our own lives. We might help them best by helping ourselves.

◆

Instead of thinking only about my children, I may need to examine the state of my own life.

In automobile terms, the child supplies the power
but the parents have to do the steering.
—*Benjamin Spock*

Our children are powerful. Their opinions are a strong
force in our lives, influencing what we eat, where we
live, where we go on vacation.

But if kids have the power, why is it parents who feel
the stress? It's because, for all their power, they still
need our "steering." They rely on our approval and our
guidance, and giving it to them around the clock wears
us down. Whether we're in the audience for our three-
year-old's puppet show, or our ninth-grader's production of *Gone With the Wind*, our involvement in our
child's life is irreplaceable.

We have to be there, boosting them, guiding them, offering our support, even when they are older. And of
course, we want to be there, too.

◆

*As I watch my child's growing sense of independence, I will
not be fooled into thinking he no longer needs me.*

Parents learn a lot from their children about coping with life.

—*Muriel Spark*

If we think about the stress in the lives of our children—peer pressure, academic pressure, the need to excel and conform—the need to be different—it may seem as if our lives are stress-free by comparison.

Many of us acknowledge this. Childhood is something we would not necessarily wish to do over again. It more than left its mark. The badge of adulthood is one of survival.

Still, we can learn a great deal by watching our children—the various ways in which they cope with everyday pressure. Their methods are creative, their spirits courageous. We would do well to imitate them.

◆

I must find a good place from which to observe my children. I will sit back, listen and learn, without judgment and without fear.

Loving a child doesn't mean giving in to all his whims: to love him is to bring out the best in him, to teach him to love what is difficult.

—*Nadia Boulanger*

Our children rarely turn to us when the going is easy. It's when the going gets tough that they call out to us.

If we rise to the occasion, if we lend her that helping hand when it is most needed, we will earn her trust, confidence, and love.

We must not give her the things she does not need. We must not make the way too easy. If we remove the struggle, we are greatly in danger of removing the life.

◆

If things seem to be going well in my child's life, I will leave well enough alone.

Showing up is 80 percent of life.

—*Woody Allen*

Sometimes we worry and fret over whether we are a potent force in our children's lives. Are we giving them enough?

But it is an absolute truth that just being there for them can often be enough. Sitting on those uncomfortable bleachers, opening the door for them after a date, applauding them as they hit their first home run, or do their first pirouette. This is really what it means to be a parent.

Just "showing up," as Woody Allen says, is often enough. Doing any more than that might be mistaken for "meddling."

◆

I take comfort in the times I have "shown up" for my children, been there when they needed me. I am proud of my participation in their lives.

Consistency requires you to be as ignorant today as you were a year ago.

—*Bernard Berenson*

We hear from the experts that to be a good parent we need to set firm limits for our children—and above all to be consistent.

Certainly this is important. Our children need to know that there is someone at the helm who knows which way is west. They need to believe that even though the game may change, the rules will stay pretty much the same. What we offer them, then, is a safe, solid base to come home to.

Still, unless we remain flexible, unless we continue to search for the answers—and maybe come up with some new solutions—we run the risk of being "as ignorant today as we were a year ago."

◆

I will think about the rules I've set down for my children to follow. If I still like what I see, I'll keep them in place. If I think they ought to be changed, I'll be flexible enough to change them.

Don't limit your child to your own learning, for he was born in another time.

—*Rabbinical saying*

If we think we are our children's sole advisers, we're bound to be exhausted by this role. We need to remind ourselves that our children will gain a great deal beyond what we can give them—and that this is a good thing.

We're struck by how often our children sound "different" to us. They seem totally comfortable with computers, take the fifty-plus stations we get on television for granted, and do not understand why "the sixties was such a big deal." They are more worried about the future of the planet than about the threat of atomic fallout.

They are different. They have different concerns, hopes, and dreams. We need to remind ourselves of this and recognize that as they explore new vistas, they are not rejecting our knowledge, they are only entering new territory of their own.

◆

I will ease my mind with the knowledge that I cannot and should not try to be the sole source of knowledge for my children.

The best brought-up children are those who have seen their parents as they are.

—*George Bernard Shaw*

When our children are allowed to see us as we really are, an incredible burden is lifted: We no longer have to hide our faults or worry about the way we are perceived. We no longer have to live up to an image we may have created for their benefit.

On the other hand, if your child believes you're Superman and finds out you're really Clark Kent, he may feel cheated, confused, and even frightened. And how will he know it's okay to have faults, okay to make mistakes, if you pretend you're invincible?

Our children need to know their real parents, not wake up one morning to find out they were the victims of an elaborate cover-up.

◆

I will make an effort to let my "real" self emerge. I will breathe easier around my children and they, in turn, will be more comfortable with me.

We have left undone those things which we ought to have done; and we have done those things which we ought not to have done.

—*Book of Common Prayer*

We may feel that, as parents, we are stuck in a rut. Every day there are sibling rivalries, schedules, and confrontations at the dinner table. We want to enjoy our children, spend time covering new ground, but the day is always "business as usual."

We may need to shake things up a bit—neglect some of those "important" errands; skip the usual routine. If we do this, our kids are bound to react suspiciously at first, but soon, they'll come to appreciate the fun in it.

Spontaneity can afford us some fine, unscripted, moments with our children. We need to inject the unpredictable into our lives and theirs.

◆

I will file away my list of "to do's" and share some spontaneous "free" time with my kids.

Insanity is hereditary. You can get it from your children.

—*Sam Levenson*

You try to be composed. You try to act as if life is manageable. But inside you feel that it is not. Everything is wild and out of control. Days spin into months, months spin into years.

Raising children can sometimes feel like a crazy experience, a whirlwind of ups and downs that leaves you with long days and little to show for them. You have to take a step back every now and then to regenerate. You may be running on empty and your children may be doing the same.

Children can go nonstop; parents can't. Maybe our children are directing our lives, setting a pace that's too fast, and we're simply too exhausted to notice.

◆

Today I will try to march to my own rhythm. I will not let my children's needs conflict with my own sense of timing.

Tomorrow is the most important thing in life. Comes into us at midnight very clean. It's perfect when it arrives and it puts itself in our hands. It hopes we've learned something from yesterday.
—*John Wayne*

Tomorrow. The clean slate. Perfectly unused, like a blank canvas waiting for the artist's brush. What a gift!

But first we have to get through today. It helps to have the knowledge that if I don't do it right, I get another chance. If I don't get it all done, I can do it tomorrow. All my yesterdays may seem riddled with mistakes— lost hours, plans gone awry. But tomorrow—that's another story. Tomorrow I get a chance to get it right!

Maybe we fear tomorrow—afraid of the new responsibilities and difficulties it might bring. Instead, we should look forward to it, trust that it will be brighter and better than today.

◆

Today I will feel better about the things I cannot accomplish because I know that tomorrow is another day.

A man should be upright, not be kept upright.
—*Marcus Aurelius*

We may feel as if we're the ones who are keeping everything going. Without us, our kids would fail. But *would* they? And if they did, would they learn something from the experience of failure?

If we're working too hard to keep our kids upright, we may need to examine our motives. We may be doing them more harm than good by smoothing the road too well, trying to create for them a perfect universe by removing the roadblocks that can offer the most important lessons of life.

If we think back to our own childhoods, it is often the failures—not the successes—that we remember most. The experiences we learn from are the ones that give us strength.

◆

I must try to remember that I cannot solve all my children's problems—and that, in fact, by doing it I may be depriving them of life's lessons.

Life is all memory except for the one present moment that goes by you so quick you hardly catch it
going.

—*Tennessee Williams*

Most of the "good stuff" of parenthood is preserved in
our memory banks. The moment, such as it is, is enjoyed, even cherished. Still, it is difficult to hang on to.
So, if we're lucky, we make time to file it away.

Sometimes, during even the busiest of days, a moment
will occur—however brief—that we know is special.
Something our child says or does, some way in which
she looks at us—and we know we must record it so it is
not lost.

True, it is nothing more than a snapshot—something
to recall in our old age. But, in light of our busy schedules, it just may be that the memory is more important
than the moment.

◆

*I will try to record the important moments as they happen.
I will understand that even if I cannot enjoy them now, I will
be able to recall them in the future.*

February 9

Always recognize that human individuals are ends, and do not use them as means to your end.
—*Immanuel Kant*

It is important to think about our children as individuals—each with his own purpose, his own sense of discovery and wonder.

They are not here to fulfill our empty lives or to find the success that eluded us. They are not here to live the life we wish we could have lived. They have a mission, a destiny, of their own. We cannot—must not—think of using them to fulfill our own misplaced dreams.

If our kids ask for our help, we can give it freely, remembering that it is our help and encouragement they seek—and not our lives.

◆

Today I will be conscience of my children as individuals, with opinions, strengths, weaknesses that differ greatly from my own.

You grow up the first time you laugh—at yourself.
—*Ethel Barrymore*

Stand back and take a good hard look at yourself as a parent and you're bound to have a good laugh or two. How did you sign on for this role? Who says you're even qualified? Sometimes it's difficult to believe we're mature enough to be "grown-ups," let alone parents.

We have to be willing to recognize the obvious: Parents are people with no training, asked to do an impossible job. Clearly, we will make mistakes. We'll look foolish at times. Even ridiculous.

We need to be able to laugh at the absurdity of it all. Only then can we say we are really "grown-up."

◆

If I feel overburdened, I will try to take the time to have a good, long laugh. If I stand back and look at my problems objectively, I may even find them amusing.

Things don't change, but by and by our wishes change.

—*Marcel Proust*

As parents, we may hope that our children grow up to look a certain way, act a certain way, think a certain way. We may want them to go to college, become professional ballplayers, study for the priesthood. Inevitably, things will not turn out the way we have wished.

But things have a way of turning out. It's not really that we alter our expectations so much as that we have a new way of looking at things. We grow. Our children grow. And life has a way of turning out the way we never could have planned it—but okay, after all.

◆

Today I will try to accept what is, and not to think about what might be or what could have been.

I wouldn't want to belong to any club that would accept me as a member.

—*Groucho Marx*

How great can a parent be, if we're allowed to be one? Are we really doing okay as parents, or are we just muddling through, doing a second-rate job?

This is one club it's safe to belong to. The guy up the street who's always out there coaching the team, or the mother on the next block who's driving her kids back and forth to school aren't really doing a better job than you are. They're just getting through the days the best way they can—even if their style is slightly different from yours.

It's a good idea to try to relax and enjoy your private membership in this very unselective club.

◆

I will use a few moments of the day to reflect upon my role as a parent—not to judge my performance, but simply to feel good about what I have accomplished.

There's always time to be late.

—*Tim Rumsey*

Any parent will tell you that lateness is a way of life. Whether you're rushing to pick up the kids from a birthday party or dropping them off at violin practice, you're bound to be late 50 percent of the time—so why not just accept it?

Maybe if we all accepted this—that timeliness isn't as important as godliness—we'd relax a little. But, too often, we're ruled by the watch, worried that if we're ten minutes late we've committed some grievous, unforgivable error.

If we can't slow ourselves down—and we should—we can at least forgive our occasional lateness. A few minutes here and there might not make all that much difference to anyone else—but it can make a world of difference in the way in which we approach our lives.

◆

Today, if I am a few minutes late, I'll understand that this is an acceptable alternative. I won't reproach myself for failing to keep up with a schedule.

Living with a saint is more grueling than being one.
—*Robert Neville*

What do we expect from our children? If they were saintlike, perfect in every way, would that make our jobs easier? If we could paint a picture of a "perfect" child, would that child be someone we'd want to live with?

Raising kids is hard work—helping them with their problems, ministering to their needs. If they were perfect, they wouldn't need us. And we'd have oh-so-much extra time on our hands—to do what with?

We mustn't expect our children to be saints—any more than we expect to see a halo every time we look in the mirror.

◆

It is comforting to help my children through a crisis. I appreciate that I am able to take part in their growth.

February 15

No one shows a child the sky.

—African proverb

These days, we're as worried about getting our kids "ready" for kindergarten as for college.

We're forgetting that children make their most exciting discoveries unassisted. An army of ants crawling in and out of an anthill; a violent thunderstorm followed by a rainbow. Educating our kids just might be as easy as opening the front door.

In this, the age of "information," it is easy to try to pour too much knowledge into our children, too soon. They may get more out of one afternoon lying under the old apple tree.

◆

Today I will forget about the planned activities, and let my children roam free for a while. It will be exciting to watch their young minds absorb the universe.

Why do grandparents and grandchildren get along so well? They have the same enemy—the mother.
—*Claudette Colbert*

Which of us hasn't envied the free-and-easy relationship our kids have with their grandparents? What makes it so appealing?

Perhaps it is the lack of expectation. As parents, we have a vested interest in our kids. If they "turn out" well, we've done a good job. If they don't, we're to blame. Grandparents know this is hogwash. They've long since realized that when it comes to raising kids most things are beyond our control, so it's best just to sit back and enjoy what you can while you can.

If we watch how the older generation acts around our children, we'll learn a valuable lesson.

◆

Today I will try to pretend my kids are someone else's. I'll let myself enjoy them, instead of expecting things from them.

If it seems a childish thing to do, do it in remembrance that you were a child.

—Frederick Buechner

Lie down. Right now. Wherever you are. Close your eyes and breathe a long sigh of relief. Pretend that no one is expecting you to be anywhere or do anything. Enjoy the moment.

This is what it's like to be a child. You were one, once. Once, you, too, had nowhere special to go, nothing special to do. The success of someone else didn't rise and fall according to your abilities. The wealth of a company didn't depend on your decisions. The health and well-being of children didn't depend on your good sense.

Even if it is for just ten minutes, be a child again.

◆

Today I will find fifteen minutes to be a child again—forgetting the responsibilities, the commitments. I will reconnect with my past.

Every form of addiction is bad, no matter whether the narcotic be alcohol or morphine or idealism.

—*Carl Jung*

Most of us begin parenthood as idealists. We really believe that if we read the right books, listen to the right advisers, trust our own basic instincts, we will raise perfect children.

It doesn't take long—maybe a month or so—before we realize how absurd this notion really is. But how do we discard it? If it is an addiction—if we're really hooked on this idealistic vision of parenthood—how do we grab hold of a more realistic view?

Perhaps we need to spend more time getting comfortable with the reality of our lives. We don't have storybook marriages—and we won't be perfect parents of perfect children. That accepted, we can go on from there.

◆

I need to remind myself that idealism can interfere with a healthy acceptance of reality.

We are all not capable of everything.

—Virgil

A parent is expected to be a cook, a teacher, a financial expert, a doctor, and a politician. If we really stop to think about how much is expected of us—how much we expect from ourselves, perhaps we may forgive ourselves for our "failures."

We're reminded of a recent conversation with a friend—a mother of three children—about to enter the workforce for the first time, but afraid that her résumé would be a blank piece of paper.

Perhaps we need to give ourselves more credit for the work that we do. We need to acknowledge that being a parent takes time, patience, and more than just a little knowledge.

◆

I must remember to congratulate myself for the work I do as a parent. I have learned a great deal and will continue to learn.

No human being can really understand another and no one can arrange another's happiness.

—*Graham Greene*

Our children don't "give" us power over their lives. Like missionaries, we come in and show them the light, then we leave them alone so they can use it.

We cannot be held responsible if they fail, any more than we can take credit if they succeed. We must try to understand that our children's lives are their own. We're happy for them, sad for them, humiliated for them, proud of them. But we are not them.

Finally, if we learn to accept this truth—that we cannot "arrange" our children's happiness—we will grow into this job.

◆

Remember, no matter how much you love your children, you are not solely responsible for their happiness.

We are making remarkable progress toward an agreement—and toward a nervous breakdown. It's going to be a race to see which will be achieved first.
—*Henry Kissinger*

We're reminded that matching wits with our kids isn't unlike Dr. Kissinger's efforts to negotiate with a foreign country.

We're viewed as "the enemy"—a threat to their independence—and they're seen as rebel forces. But strong-arming doesn't work. Using tact and diplomacy does. Giving in on some issues, we will gain on others. And slowly, after years of patience and perseverance, we will achieve the peace we are seeking.

◆

To see things from my child's point of view does not mean I am "giving in." To promote peace, the opposition needs to be heard.

There's nothing quite so valuable as work. That's why it's a good idea to leave some for tomorrow.
—*Marian Dolliver*

We don't have to get everything done today. Whether it's a stack of work on our desks or a pile of laundry, it can wait until tomorrow.

But if we put it off till tomorrow, we need to forget about it—completely—until then. That's the hard part. Getting rid of the guilt, the anxiety. We don't want to bring it to the tennis court or to the lake or to a concert. We don't want it hanging over us as we sit down on the floor to build Legos with our kids.

If we get away from our work—mentally and physically—we will come back to it fresher, remembering its importance in our lives.

◆

When I don't get away from my work, I am really diminishing its importance in my life. Getting away from work is not a gift I give myself. It is my right.

Love is an act of endless forgiveness, a tender look which becomes a habit.

—*Peter Ustinov*

In day-to-day parenting, we sometimes forget that love is a process. We may feel incredible anger toward our children, but we do not stop loving them.

We have to understand that these feelings we have are normal and acceptable. We're too hard on ourselves, always expecting to feel total love and compassion. We are in the "habit" of loving our children, because we endlessly forgive them their misbehaviors. This does not mean that we love them every moment of every day.

When rage turns to abuse, it is because healthy expression of anger is denied.

◆

I will allow myself to feel angry toward my children when it is justified. I will understand that these feelings are acceptable.

Life would give her everything of consequence. Life would shape her, not we. All we were good for was to make the introductions.

—*Helen Hayes*

This is the catch-22 of parenting: We are responsible for giving our children life, but from that moment forward, life takes over and we don't have a whole lot to say about it.

We make rules only to have them broken. We espouse values only to have them challenged. We provide limits only to have them tested—repeatedly.

Still, we are here. Like the guide who leads a traveler through the wilderness, we are here, with our skills and our knowledge and our experience, ready to lead the way. But the experience is theirs. It is life that will shape them, not we.

◆

Our children need to live their own lives and will do so, whether or not they have our approval.

I talk and talk and talk, and I haven't taught people in fifty years what my father taught by example in one week.

—*Mario Cuomo*

You can talk to your kids until their eyes glaze over, and it probably won't mean a thing. Kids don't learn from what you say—they learn from what you do.

The irony is that you're losing control of your own life, while you're trying to help them lead theirs. This is something to think about. If you take time to put your own affairs in order, to make your own life more valuable, aren't you teaching your kids something about responsibility?

Think of the things you learned from your parents. Do you remember what they said or what they did?

◆

I show my kids more by being a responsible, caring member of society than by leading a life that is totally devoted to their welfare.

You have a wonderful child. Then, when he's thirteen, gremlins carry him away and leave in his place a stranger who gives you not a moment's peace.
—*Jill Eikenberry*

No matter how much we do, we can't change the fact that sooner or later our kids will grow up, demand independence—and get it. We may as well make up our minds to grant it willingly—unless we want a large-scale rebellion on our hands.

It helps to be prepared. We need to keep in mind, from the first moment we see that beautiful infant, that she will someday have a life of her own. When she's a toddler, we need to encourage, not thwart, her efforts toward independence. And when she's a teenager, her being able to stand alone in the world, on her own two feet, is our reward, not our punishment.

If we push really hard against our child's independent spirit, we may be locked in combat for good.

♦

It is up to me to recognize my child's need for independence. I will have her respect if I grant her my respect.

The beauty of "spacing" children many years apart lies in the fact that parents have time to learn the mistakes that were made with the older ones—which permits them to make exactly the opposite mistakes with the younger ones.

—*Sydney J. Harris*

Just because we do things "differently" with the second and third child doesn't mean we do them better. We're bound to make mistakes with each and learn from each.

Doing it over and over doesn't mean getting it "right." There is no "right" in parenting, just as there is no "wrong." We need to know and accept this so that we can relax and let our instincts carry us forward. Otherwise, our own insecurity is passed on to our children and our children's children.

◆

It makes perfect sense that we will react differently with each of our children; children are people, with their own set of needs and behaviors.

Sleep is the best meditation.

—*Dalai Lama*

Sleep. The one thing parents, especially new parents, get little of. The one thing we do not know is precious until the first night we lose it.

It's part of the survival code of new parents—the badge of honor. How little we sleep determines whether or not we are doing the job well. Wrong! If we're martyrs—if we think we can survive without sleep—we will soon learn that this kind of deprivation can lead to illness and frustration.

Sleep is restorative. It gives us the energy to go on. It helps us see things in a new light. We cannot do without it. We must not try.

◆

I will get more sleep tonight. My body needs rest. My mind needs to be recharged.

Never lend your car to anyone to whom you have given birth.

—*Erma Bombeck*

Teenagers and your brand-new Ford Explorer don't mix. Neither does a birthday party full of six-year-olds and the light beige living room carpet.

If you have to worry about whether or not your kids are going to destroy your possessions, you ought to remove the likelihood. Some of your things are just that—your things. This is okay. You don't have to share everything with your son or daughter.

Co-habitation requires boundaries. You don't read your thirteen-year-old's diary; she doesn't borrow your necklace without permission. You can live together if there's respect on both sides.

◆

Teaching your children about boundaries is as important as teaching them about self-respect.

We are always getting ready to live but never living.
—*Ralph Waldo Emerson*

Forever on the brink. The diver, waiting, poised above the water. The hunter, rifle aimed, hand on the trigger, eye on the target. And parents. Ready, waiting. For what? A distant prize? Some future reward?

The moment is now. This is our reward. Every time our child greets us; every time we tuck him in at night. These are the moments that are the joys of parenthood. We need to live them to the fullest, knowing they may be all we get.

Our lives pass us by if we do not live in the present. We live in process, fueled by our disease, spurred on by our weaknesses. This is living.

◆

What we have at the moment is ours to enjoy. The future may bring other rewards, but we cannot count on them.

The most decisive actions of our life—I mean those that are most likely to decide the whole course of our future—are more often than not, unconsidered.

—*André Gide*

If there's a trick to it, maybe it's called "spontaneity." Keep things fluid and flexible. Don't make too many plans or look too far ahead, and you'll be all right.

Parenting, like life itself, requires us to take a back seat to happenstance. Things will just happen, whether we wish them to or not. We cannot prevent or predict the future; so we may as well make up our minds to accept it.

Planning has its place; but we should never become so attached to the prescribed route that we lose our ability to examine a sudden fork in the road.

◆

I feel lighter when I embrace the future and do not try to control it. Let me face the day without a prescribed plan and see what comes up.

Decide promptly but never give any reasons. Your decisions may be right, but your reasons are sure to be wrong.

—*Lord Mansfield*

Let's face it. Our children don't usually settle for "yes" or "no" answers. They want an explanation. *Why* can't I stay out till midnight? *Why* can't I turn my jeans into shorts? *Why* can't I have a new bicycle?

Don't be fooled. It's a trap—designed to see if parents will fall for it. A conspiracy of sorts. You see, your kids know you haven't really thought it through and you're unsure about the reason, even if you have one. They'll try to drag a reason out of you, but if you're smart, you won't fall for it.

Does this sound unfair? Don't we owe our kids an explanation? Emphatically, resoundingly, no. We do not.

◆

I am learning to make decisions quickly and to live with the consequences.

The way positive reinforcement is carried out is more important than the amount.

—B. F. Skinner

When praising your kids, it's better not to overdo it. Too much praise can be as damaging as too little.

Kids respond to a kind word here and there—and to a reward they know is really deserved. But they'll begin to tune it out if it comes loud and often. They know the difference between a gratuitous gesture and a heartfelt hug.

Some parents feel guilty if they do not spend enough time praising their kids. This is totally unjustified.

◆

I reinforce my children by praising them when they deserve to be praised. They, in turn, respect my sincerity.

When do any of us ever do enough?
—*Barbara Jordan*

What is the measure of success? A high-paying job? A healthy, loving family? Lots of friends? How do we judge when we've reached the top, assuming that's what we're aiming for? How do we know when we have all we really need?

The truth is, it's difficult to set our own quotas. We're not really sure what we're aiming for, so it's difficult to know when we reach our mark. Perhaps we need to be clearer about our goals, so that we can feel some measure of pride and gratitude when we reach them.

Doing "enough" instead of doing "too much" means we have to know what "enough" is. Each of us needs to set up a signpost, so we'll recognize "enough" when we get there.

◆

I can stop when I get there if I know where "there" is. Today I'll spend some time thinking about the goals I have set for myself.

The right to be heard does not automatically include the right to be taken seriously.
—*Hubert H. Humphrey*

If we can't understand why our kids aren't listening to us, maybe we need to examine what it is we're saying.

Our kids have their own ideas which, no doubt, will differ radically from our own. We can't automatically assume they'll adopt our beliefs. They may have values and beliefs of their own. We can't automatically assume they will subscribe to our principles. They are, daily, developing principles of their own.

They'll hear what we say and then choose for themselves. This is their right. This is as it should be.

◆

I will tell my children how I feel about things, but I will not expect them to feel the same way.

Parents were invented to make children happy by giving them something to ignore.

—*Ogden Nash*

Of course you are important to your kids. But not so important that they can't ignore 75 percent of what you say. Not so important that they can't take you for granted. Not so important that they wouldn't trade you for—say—an autographed baseball.

Seriously, though, maybe we need to see things in the right perspective. Sure, we're important to our kids. In fact, we're indispensable. But let's not be so smug as to think they can't ever get along without us.

Our children are happiest when they know we'll be there for them—if and when they need us.

◆

Your child's happiness does not depend on being with you every waking hour.

There is no more miserable human being than one in whom nothing is habitual but indecision.
—*William James*

Parenting involves a high degree of risk. Every time you make a decision there is a chance—a good one—that you'll make the wrong one.

So what? If you make the decision, stick by it. Indecision is like the horse that never gets out of the starting gate—it hasn't got a prayer of winning the race. At least, if you make a decision, you have a fifty-fifty chance of making the right one. (And give yourself even better odds if it's your second child. We all make more mistakes with the first).

Indecision breeds more indecision. Feel confident, and you'll pass that confidence along to your kids.

◆

It will help my kids to act decisively in their world if I can do the same in mine.

Sacrifice is a form of bargaining.

—*Holbrook Jackson*

If we think of what we have given up for our children—the things we might have been able to afford, the places we could have gone, the career we postponed—it may seem as if we have sacrificed a great deal.

But if we think of parenting as a sacrifice, how do we expect our children to repay it? What do we expect from them in return? We certainly cannot expect them to replace what we have lost. It's important for us to understand that parenting is a choice we have made, not a bargaining tool.

As parents, we must think of what we have gained, not what we have lost. Parenting is not sacrifice; it is reward.

◆

When it comes to my children, I have no hidden agendas. What I do for them, I do freely and lovingly, with no expectation of repayment.

Life must be understood backward. But—it must be lived forward.

—*Søren Kierkegaard*

Parenting is a road we travel. There are no signposts, no mileage markers. We set the speed limit—and most of the time we find ourselves going too fast. We're not sure where the road leads, but we have the feeling we'll know where we're going when we get there.

This is a journey we make alone—a pilgrimage of sorts. Sometimes it is as if we are in a dream where nothing makes sense. Just when we feel secure, at peace, things change. Just when we think we know our children, they grow older and seem strange to us. We are outsiders in their world—a world we used to find comfortingly familiar.

For now, we must continue forward on this journey. It will make sense to us only when it is over, when we look back.

◆

I will try to face each day with a positive outlook, secure in the knowledge that what I do not understand today I may understand tomorrow.

When you have got an elephant by the hind legs
and he is trying to run away, it's best to let him run.
—*Abraham Lincoln*

There's a force you are trying to reckon with that all
parents before you—and all who come later—meet.

Youth is powerful. It fights for its freedom. It does not
want to be held back. If you fight against it, you will
undoubtedly lose. Parents who do too much to resist it
may end up facing a full-scale rebellion when their
kids reach teenage.

You probably want to hold on for dear life, but sooner
or later you'll learn that it's better to let the elephant
run.

◆

*I need to give my children a chance to lead their own lives.
If I allow them to break free, I'll also give myself greater freedom.*

Our chief want in life is somebody who will make us do what we can.

—*Ralph Waldo Emerson*

Maybe what we really need to be for our children is a mirror: We show them their true selves by holding up a reflection of their potential.

Our kids will have doubts and fears. They will struggle with self-worth and self-doubt. But they look in the mirror that we hold before them and see hope. They see that we have faith in them, and they will be able to go on.

If all we provide for our children is the inspiration to lead a full life, to live up to their potential, we are doing a lot. We don't need to interpret life for them; but we do need to show them what is innately possible.

◆

If I do nothing more for my kids than offer them support, I am doing a lot. I will try to be their mirror and their sounding board.

Today's timely question: How do you explain coun-
terclockwise to a youngster with a digital watch?
—*Anonymous*

The truth is, one generation doesn't learn a whole lot
from the generation that came before. What we pass
on to our children is the result of economic failures or
successes, our careful or careless use of the environment, our technological and industrial advances. These
are things our children are stuck with—for good or
ill—and will make the best or worst of in their own
time.

But a meeting of the minds may never occur. We may
never fully understand them, nor they us. It may be futile to try.

◆

*I will try to recognize that my children are of a new gener-
ation and that sometimes we may speak a different language.*

The surest way to make it hard for children is to make it easy for them.

—*Eleanor Roosevelt*

If we do too much for our children, we may be depriving them of life. If our children are never allowed to experience struggle, if they are never allowed to know fear, they may never be able to face death. If we create for them a "perfect" existence, we are narrowing their possibilities and robbing them of their free will.

It is natural for us to want our children to lead smooth lives, free of pain and sorrow. But we must recognize that without these things life does not exist. A life without suffering may also be a life without joy.

◆

Doing everything for my children is doing too much. They are strong enough to face whatever crises and challenges they must face in the future.

Children whom suburban life was supposed to make wholesome little Johns and Wendys became the acid-dropping, classroom-burning hippies of the 1960s.
—*Ronald Steel*

If there is anything we learned from our own parents, it is that their money did not buy our happiness. Even if they provided us with the best education that money could buy, there was no guarantee they bought us a bright future.

Likewise, if your child grows up in a two-room cottage, without all the advantages, it doesn't mean he cannot become successful. The history books are filled with success stories that could never have been predicted—men and women who have risen above their circumstances, above what was expected of them or what could have been predicted for them.

Don't think you have to buy your kids success. No matter how much you give them, they will take only what they need and grow into whatever they are destined to become.

◆

I need to remember that my children will not turn out as expected. The results will surprise me, whatever they may be.

You don't raise heroes, you raise sons. And if you treat them like sons, they'll turn out to be heroes, even if it's just in your own eyes.

—*Walter M. Schirra, Sr.*

We can and will have dreams for our kids; but we can't expect them to live up to our dreams. On the other hand, if we treat our kids fairly, with love and respect, we can almost guarantee they will live up to their own dreams.

If you think back to when your first child was born, you'll undoubtedly remember the magic of that new life. A child so filled with promise for the future. Perhaps you were afraid that if you made a mistake—even a simple one—it would scar her for life.

The truth is, there is room for imperfection, as long as there is love. Our kids won't be perfect, but who is?

◆

I can't raise my children to be heroes or presidents or saints. I have to recognize the beauty that lies in imperfection and the pride that accompanies growth.

The important thing is not so much that every child should be taught, as that every child should be given the wish to learn.

—*John Lubbock*

If your child asks you a lot of questions, now might be the time to offer yourself a pat on the back. Somewhere along the way, you've given him the wish to learn, and this is a wonderful thing.

Sure, you're busy. It's tough to take time away from washing the car, answering the phone, going to the bank, to stop and explain to your eight-year-old that the horizon is an imaginary line. But, it's worth the effort. This is your child, after all. When you answer his questions, you encourage him to ask more questions, and, finally, to think for himself.

We need to take time out from our busy schedules to answer these all-important questions that are put to us by our children. They may be the most important questions we answer today.

◆

I help my child more by answering his questions than by freely dispensing my advice.

Many a time I have wanted to stop talking and find out what I really believed.

—*Walter Lippmann*

We get used to the sound of our own voice. It is reassuring, but sometimes maddeningly foolish. We say things we wish we hadn't said, reveal things we wish we had kept to ourselves. The words are out of our mouths before we are sure we believe them.

How do we get in touch with what we believe, when we are so busy, our lives so complicated? There is an urge to communicate at all costs—to make ourselves known. But we risk sharing pieces of the puzzle before the puzzle is complete. We risk putting ourselves, our opinions, out into the world before they are fully formed.

If we want to be sure that what we say to our children is what we really mean, we need to listen to our inner voices before we speak. We need to begin to like what we hear ourselves saying.

◆

Listening to my inner voice may give me important clues about how I really feel, what I really believe. I will learn how to think before I speak.

I wanted it to be a fresh start, for you to be more complete than we had ever been ourselves, but I wonder if we expected too much.

—*Richard Olton*

The family may be a unit, but each of its parts has to be whole. Your spouse doesn't complete you. Your children don't complete you. You complete you.

If this isn't clear, think about a tree, its branches reaching upward toward the sky. The trunk is the family, sturdy and strong, its roots deep. The branches are you and your children, all reaching separately upward. Each of you is strong. Maybe you could bend or break in a strong wind, but the trunk supports you, prevents you from snapping.

This is your family. Each of you is complete, separate, whole. You depend on one another for strength and support, and you do not expect from one another more than you can give.

◆

My children are whole and separate from me. I do not complete them and I will not try to.

Oh what a tangled web we weave when first we practice to conceive.

—*Don Herold*

Is parenting all it's cracked up to be—or some elaborate trick we play on ourselves? Do we get what we wished for?

If it's a joke, it's an elaborate one. It's filled with emotion and glory, pain and sorrow. It summons from us our greatest strengths and our greatest fears. It causes us to reach down inside ourselves to places we've long forgotten, and pull out extraordinary riches.

We thought we would have a couple of kids. We gave ourselves enormous challenge, pleasure, and pain.

◆

If parenting is not what I thought it would be, I will try to accept it for what it is. I am growing as my children grow.

Many who have spent a lifetime in it can tell us less of love than the child that lost a dog yesterday.
—*Thornton Wilder*

Maybe we don't give our kids credit for deep, complex emotion. If they are in pain, we may try to ease their burden, never suspecting that they are capable of working it out for themselves.

But children can and do feel deeply about things. They may shrug it off and start over, but this does not mean they don't think about it for some time. If, on the other hand, you try to take away their pain, you may be removing their ability to cope—permanently.

Your children need your consolation; but you do not need to loan them your strength. They have their own strength and need to learn how to use it.

◆

Remember, your child has the ability to connect with his own pain. He will find his own strength, too, if you let him.

Many a man wishes he were strong enough to tear a telephone book in half—especially if he has a teenage daughter.

—*Guy Lombardo*

How many times have we wanted to be superhuman for our sons and daughters? But we have strengths and weaknesses, and regardless of how much we may wish to appear immortal, our kids will soon discover that we are not.

We need to concentrate on being strong for ourselves, not for our children. If we are in good shape—reasonably sound health, financially comfortable, emotionally secure, our kids will reap the benefits. Our children do not need us to be supermen and superwomen. They do need us to feel good about ourselves.

When we do sacrifice our leisure time, wallow in self-pity, or engage in other destructive behaviors, we are robbing our children of the right to healthy parents. Protecting ourselves, nurturing ourselves—these are things we do in our children's best interests.

◆

If I want my children to be proud of my strength, I need to be smart about the way I live my life. If I take care of myself, I will be strong for my children.

The car trip can draw the family together, as it was in the days before television, when parents and children actually talked to each other.

—*Andrew H. Malcolm*

We may do more than we have to do and talk to our children less than we should. If we find creative ways of being together—even if it's only for an hour a day—we may give ourselves a great gift. But we've become a generation of television junkies, glued to the mesmerizing, all-powerful box and its tantalizing array of goodies. We sit before it, worshiping its bounty, afraid that if it were to break down, so would we.

It's time to replace the twenty-seven-inch screen with some good old-fashioned conversation. My kids may have more to offer me this evening than the six o'clock news.

◆

I'll put aside the remote control today and spend those extra moments with my children.

He vanished to the public in order to materialize for his family.

—*Lance Morrow*

Must we sacrifice our time at work in order to give more time to our families? Or is it possible to divide our time between them, giving each our best?

Some people say that it is possible. We can burn the candle at both ends. We can have it all. Others say it is impossible. We cannot expect to be good enough mothers and fathers and also get accolades in our profession. Maybe we have to settle for a less demanding job, or for less involvement with our children. One or the other.

There is a choice and it is ours to make. But one thing is clear: if we wish to take a step back from our careers in order to spend more time with our families, we should not be punished for it.

◆

I need to remain open to the possibilities: If I must slow down somewhat in my career, I will try not to feel guilty about it.

Choice is tyranny.

—*Jonathon Lazear*

Of course our children need choices. But if we give them too many, we may be inviting disaster.

Was it simpler when we were kids or does it just seem that way? Did we have as many options as we've given them? Our children need us to keep the umbrella over their heads—at least for a while. We should offer them a choice, but make the choice clear. "Do you want to do this—or that?" Not "What do you want to do?"

If we remember what it was like to be children, it will make it easier for us to be parents. We will remember the safety of boundaries, the reassurance of limits. We will recall how thrilling it was to be free—when we knew our parents were waiting around the corner.

◆

My children need me to provide reasonable choices for them to make; they also need me to set reasonable limits.

Find the grain of truth in criticism—chew it and swallow it.

—*D. Sutten*

The answers are all around us, if we choose to look and listen. We hear the voices of our parents, of our grandparents, of our sisters and brothers. We hear the voices of experts and novices, of friends and strangers. We learn from those who have come before us and those who came before them.

Parenting is not new. It is all around us in the ideas, feelings, attitudes of others who are just like us. We can learn from them, if we are not afraid to learn. Maybe they have something important to tell us: one grain of truth, one important bit of information.

Our instincts are good, but we may also learn from others. We need to process the information that comes to us, take what is good, and discard the rest.

◆

There may be something important someone is trying to tell me today; I will keep my eyes and ears open for this message.

I never promised you a rose garden.
—*Hannah Green*

When you sign on as a parent, you can expect thorns to come up with the roses. The true course of parenting doesn't run smooth. Your kids will challenge you, motivate you, frighten you, drive you crazy. They will definitely change your life for good. If you are ready for this change, it will be positive. If you fight it, get ready for a bumpy ride.

Remember, there are no signs on this freeway. Even if you know there will be twists and turns in the road ahead, you still need to hang on tight.

◆

Facing the challenges of parenthood will make me stronger. I cannot predict the future, but I can be prepared to face it.

We discover our parents when we become parents ourselves.

—*Anonymous*

We may not have thought they had much to teach us; then, suddenly we are parents and we find ourselves wanting to reconnect with our own parents.

We need to allow ourselves to do this. There is a great deal we can learn from our parents, even though times have changed. We may find some of their methods old-fashioned, their ideas out of date, but they can teach us about perspective and courage. If they came through it, so can we.

Our parents may not have been as busy as we are. But they lived through war and depression. They can teach us how to survive, because they were survivors.

◆

Hearing what my parents have to say may be just the right antidote for a difficult day.

Hope is the feeling you have that the feeling you have isn't permanent.

—*Jean Kerr*

It's the end of a long day, but you've gotten through it. Your kids needed you, your boss needed you, your spouse needed you. Once again, you've had no time for yourself.

The good news is, things change. No matter how the walls seem to be closing in, tomorrow is filled with promise.

One of the best things about parenting is that it's not a static situation. Our children grow and change, as we do. Daily, we get another chance.

◆

In the future, there is hope and the possibility for growth and change. I will keep an eye out for it.

> You can't have everything. Where would you put it?
> —*Steven Wright*

Is there ever an end to what we wish for? Or do we always have the secret hope that some day we will have everything? If we did have everything, could we use it? We would, supposedly, lack for nothing. But having everything gives you time for nothing.

Having everything might be the curse of all time. It might be the worst thing that could happen to us. Having everything would not give us time to do the things we most love to do. And, maybe worst of all, it would mean we would never have the need to dream, a most satisfying occupation.

We need to recognize and understand and accept the concept of "enough." We need to give ourselves permission to stop wanting more.

◆

I certainly do not have everything I ever wanted, but I can be satisfied with what I have.

The best way out is always through.

—*Robert Frost*

Frost did a lot of talking about "roads." The one "not taken." The ones that "converged in a wood." He understood that "the path" is a symbol we can relate to. We all feel comfortable with the knowledge that we're on a journey. We see life that way.

He saw, too, that life could only be really lived by living it. If you're going to get tired and sit down in the middle of the road, you're never going to see what's at the end of the road. If you see every experience as a make-or-break situation, you'll be defeated by your own shortsightedness. You've got to walk right through parenthood with your best intentions in your back pocket and your head held high. Walk straight down the road and you'll find your own way.

◆

When I understand that parenthood is a journey, I give myself permission to learn from the experience.

Never help a child with a task at which he feels he can succeed.

—*Maria Montessori*

The key words from this brilliant educator are "he feels he can succeed." Not "you" but "he."

Basically, your child knows what he's capable of. You may not. You may think you know—but the truth may surprise you. Have you ever watched an idle dog in a yard? If he thinks no one is looking, he finds plenty to do. But pay him any attention at all, and he's all over you, waiting for your next command.

It's the same with children. Give them half a chance and they'll surprise you with their ingenuity and ability. But climb all over them with suggestions and support, and they'll probably let you. "You do it," they'll say. And you will.

If your child "feels he can succeed," give him a chance. In this case, doing too much means doing what he could have done just as well or better.

◆

When I take over for my children, they don't experience the joy of success. I will give them the freedom to do what they are able to do without my assistance.

A child's hand in yours—what tenderness it arouses, what power it conjures. You are instantly the very touchstone of wisdom and strength.

—*Marjorie Holmes*

Parenting is heady stuff. When your child smiles up at you, holds your hand with pride, or brags about your accomplishments, it gives you a feeling of incredible power.

It can also be a burden. Many of us find it difficult to live up to the image our child has of us, especially if it is radically different from our own self-image.

Pretend you have the lead role in a play. You are a king. This is how your child sees you. You are uneasy with a crown atop your head, but you recognize that this is the most important role you will ever play.

◆

I try to live up to my children's expectations, but I know I can't please them 100 percent of the time.

April 4

People should think less about what they ought to do and more about what they ought to be. If only their living were good, their work would shine forth brightly.

—*Meister Eckhart*

We may ask our children, "What do you want to be when you grow up?" when we really mean, "What do you want to do?" The answer to the first question might be: "A good person." "An intellectual." "An idealist." "A dreamer." But as we teach our children, in and out of school, we are looking for scientists, doctors, lawyers. We ask them to study a subject, not to study life.

As parents, we need only regard our children (and ourselves, for that matter) as people aspiring to live well. If we live well, we have the potential to "do" well. If we are true to ourselves, passionate about our causes, deliberate in our attitudes, connected to our thoughts, and kind to others, then we will "do well."

◆

I need to learn that there is a difference between what I do and who I am. I need to pass this truth on to my children.

Two persons must believe in each other, and feel that it can be done and must be done; in that way they are enormously strong. They must keep each other's courage.

—*Vincent van Gogh*

These words can just as easily apply to parenthood as to a marriage. The relationship between you and your child can be like a marriage—a bond of strength and mutual faith. You lend your child your support and she, in turn, gives you her faith in your ability to lead her. Your success is dependent on both of you together.

Maybe, as a parent, you see yourself as the strong one, and your child as the dependent. Certainly this is true to some degree. But it's also true that there are times when you can lean on your children, depend on their strength and courage. This isn't a sign of weakness or of immaturity. It's a sign of honesty—and, sometimes, a means of survival. You teach your child to stay afloat in rough waters—and he comes back to save you when you're drowning.

◆

I must remember that parenthood is a give-and-take relationship. If I do all the giving, I am denying my children the right to give back.

A p r i l 6

Why don't you get a haircut? You look like a chrysanthemum.

—*P. G. Wodehouse*

If only we could see our teenagers as they see themselves, these years might be easier. But this is, after all, a battle as old as time itself. It is their turn to express themselves, and there's just no way you're going to see eye to eye with them, even if they've reached your height—or taller.

So you look at their latest haircut or outfit and wring your hands in despair. What can you do? If you engage them in battle, you'll be seen as "the enemy" and you'll probably lose the war even if you win the battle.

It's hard to remember the really important things when you're being challenged by your teenager. You have to try to keep your wits about you and remember that the less you say, the wiser you may appear.

◆

Maybe there are times when my children will respect my silence more than my advice.

The only thing more difficult than following a regimen is not imposing it on others.

—*Marcel Proust*

Just because you've earned the right to vote, to hold a job, to own a house and to have kids, doesn't mean you've earned the right to tell everyone else how to live. You've gotten there, and you're proud of it. But everyone else—including your kids—needs to arrive there—wherever "there" is—on his own steam.

It's hard to remember this, but it's important: We all have our own agendas, our own life plans. If you had someone else's map, you'd get lost. You need to follow your own. Your kids do, too. What you can do for them is let them. Be there, as needed, but let them make mistakes, get lost, lose direction and find it again. Let them go at their own pace. They are trying, just as you did, to carve a path for themselves. They are not trying to follow yours.

◆

I can give my kids a start in life, but I cannot impose my own life plan on them.

April 8

> We've had bad luck with our kids—they've all grown up.
>
> —*Christopher Morley*

Funny thing about childhood: It passes. We all grow up. Only Peter Pan could stay young forever, and he had a heck of a time trying. In the end, even Peter was worn out.

Whatever you do as a parent, you cannot prevent the inevitable: Your kids will turn into adults. They will do this whether you spoil them, baby them, bribe them, or beg them. They will do this whether you praise them, punish them, stifle them, or set them free. Children grow up.

One thing we need to recognize as parents is that despite our efforts, despite the worrying, the planning, the hard work we do, our kids will "turn out" to be whatever they can be or should be or want to be. Our kids will turn into adults.

◆

I need to allow my children to grow up, even if it means their needing me less.

Everybody gets so much common information all day long that they lose their common sense.

—*Gertrude Stein*

In our society, parents have no shortage of information: We have books, tapes, television shows, seminars, and videos. There may be no guidelines, but there certainly are enough guides and gurus to go around.

Sometimes our instinct shouts a response that rises above the din. If we listen, we can just about hear it. We need to follow that voice. It is telling us the right answer, the one that comes from deep inside us. We have a gut feeling that is correct—a basic instinct that springs from love itself. These are our children, and, deep down, we know what is best for them.

Parenting is even more difficult when we turn in so many different directions. We can make our lives easier by getting back in touch with our true selves.

◆

I need to spend some time away from the crowd. I can and must begin to rely on my own instincts.

The day is of infinite length for him who knows how to appreciate and use it.

—*Johann Wolfgang von Goethe*

How you spend your time is up to you. You can run around in circles all day long, investing yourself in a hundred different activities, challenging yourself in a thousand ways. Or you can choose your challenges, letting your judgment guide you through the maze of opportunity.

Finding the life within your life does not mean squeezing the last ounce out of each day. Sometimes you must distance yourself from activity in order to recognize the real opportunity; you must refuse the challenge in order to find the hidden gifts.

◆

I know I am too heavily invested and need to examine my overcommitment. Doing less does not necessarily mean getting less out of life.

If the world were merely seductive, that would be easy. If it were merely challenging, that would be no problem. But I arise on the morning torn between a desire to improve (or save) the world and a desire to enjoy (or savor) the world. This makes it hard to plan the day.

—*E. B. White*

On a scale of one to ten, where do we place enjoyment? Do we have time to "enjoy" our children? Can we, "savor" them or are we too busy "saving" them?

From a distance, it is easy to see that enjoyment counts. What is the reason for creation, if not to enjoy it? What is the reason for having children, if not spend time with them? But, in reality, enjoyment has taken a back seat to the "necessities" of life. We are frantically busy "providing" for our kids: food, clothing, education. We rarely have time to "provide" them with ourselves.

The dilemma is not easily solved. Enjoyment has to fit in our schedules like everything else. But we need to know that there is a place for it. And it is not last.

◆

Today I will give myself permission to take time to enjoy my children, even if it does not easily fit into the schedule.

A p r i l   1 2

Middle age: When you are sitting at home on Saturday night and the telephone rings and you hope it isn't for you.

—*Ring Lardner*

There was a time when you were the one going to the rock concert, hanging out at the diner, cheering at the football game. There was a time when these things were more important to you than anything else. Now, what may be more important than anything else is a good night's rest—a vacation from the pressures of life.

It is difficult to understand how this happened: how you acquired this need for solitude. But when you are a parent, you give—constantly—and you can only restore yourself when you are by yourself. You need to find this peace—to give yourself permission to have it.

When the phone rings on Saturday night—let it ring. Refuse to answer it. Give yourself permission to rest.

◆

It is not possible to be a parent without having time to rest. I need to give myself permission to be by myself.

Nothing grows well in the shade of a big tree.
—*Constantin Brancusi*

As you tend your garden, you make sure it has water and sunlight. Carefully, you pull the weeds. You fertilize it, and spray it to discourage harmful insects. Then, you leave it alone for a while. You sit back and watch your garden grow and flourish.

Our kids need the same kind of tending as our gardens. They need us to do "enough" for them so that they can grow and flourish. They do not need us to do too much. When we hover over our children, they feel trapped. They love us and need us but they do not want to be overtended. They need room to grow.

This is a boundary issue, but it's also about respect. If you love and respect your children, you'll give them plenty of space in which to grow.

◆

To love is to leave alone occasionally. My children need to know that I am here, but do not need me to block the sun.

We are shaped and fashioned by what we love.
—*Johann Wolfgang von Goethe*

Perhaps this is a good time to stop and think about what we get out of being parents. Yes, we do a lot. We do too much. Our lives are nightmarishly busy. But we also get a lot. The love we have for our children recreates us, makes us new every day.

Parenting forever changes us. Fashioned by the children we love, we turn into different people. We might not recognize ourselves if we were to look back. We might see ourselves, at the start of this enterprise, as selfish people, people with small, predictable lives.

Our lives are busier now, but they have meaning. Our lives are puzzling now, but they are alive with possibility. Our children have reinvented us.

◆

I am grateful for the changes my children have brought about in me.

There is more to life than increasing its speed.
—*Mahatma Gandhi*

You'd never know this by the way we live. We are frantic these days. Christmas catalogues appear in July. We're researching colleges while our kids are still in elementary school. We're always pushing ourselves to do more and faster.

"Faster" has not given us a better life. "Faster" has only given us ulcers and heart attacks. The speed at which we work—or play—is not directly proportionate to our enjoyment. Why, then, are we on overdrive? What is it that dictates this pace? Perhaps we are afraid that if we slow down we'll be left behind. Our neighbors, friends, cousins, colleagues will outrun us.

Maybe we need to start realizing that there is more to be gained by "looking around" than by forging ahead. And who knows? From "behind" we just might have a better view.

◆

I can gain a great deal today by slowing down, looking around, and giving myself a chance to reap what I've sown.

A p r i l   1 6

Guilt is the Mafia of the mind.

—*Bob Mandel*

What we don't do—what we can't get done—overwhelms us, even terrorizes us. This is dangerous. As parents, we must not allow guilt to prevail.

There are days when we feel gloriously in control, capable of succeeding on all levels of our lives. We are on top of things, and the hours seem to go by according to our script. But when we are out of control, when we are tyrannized by the clock, our script falls apart. There are miscues and false starts. Our plans go awry. We feel tremendous guilt because we allowed ourselves to fail.

We cannot blame ourselves when the course of a day does not run smoothly. Some days have surprises in store, and we need to be flexible enough to allow events to happen. Control is elusive. But guilt can ruin an otherwise acceptable day.

◆

If I am overly programmed, ruled by my own master plan, I am bound to experience frustration and guilt. I need to relax my standards.

After all, what is reality anyway? Nothin' but a collective hunch.

—*Jane Wagner*

It's time we faced facts. Parenthood is guesswork. The two are synonymous. No one—not our neighbors down the street or our parents or our brothers-in-law—has the prescription for success. It all looks good from the outside, but if we lived in their houses, we'd know the truth: We're all doing this by the seat of our pants.

So let your hunches rule. Treat your guesses like honored guests. Sooner or later, you will realize that they are not last-minute invitees.

It is only when you acknowledge that spontaneity is best—that you can accomplish more as a parent by trusting your instincts—that you will begin to enjoy this job.

◆

I'll go with my hunches today, pay attention to my instincts. This is my only reality.

The only Zen you find on the top of mountains is the Zen you bring up there.

—*Robert M. Pirsig*

If you are searching for answers, remember to look within. In parenting, you are likely to find that you are your own best guide, the one who has the solution.

If you are busy looking all around you—seeking solutions from other sources—you may miss what has been there all along. You can go to the top of the mountain and beyond, but if you won't or can't acknowledge what's inside you, how can you pass anything worthwhile along to your children? Your children need *you*. The most wonderful thing you can give them is the part of yourself you have been reluctant to reveal.

Remember that all of us have something that is worth giving. Our children will learn more from us if we are open and give ourselves freely—than if we buy them the best education money can buy.

◆

I have something worthwhile to impart to my children. Today I will open myself up to them.

Intensity is so much more becoming in the young.
—*Joanne Woodward*

Trying too hard is wearing us down. We cannot be endlessly imaginative, creative, brilliant. We cannot take total responsibility for enriching our children's lives. It is exhausting and even wears our children down.

Some days we can almost feel the intensity. It is overwhelming. We want to do it all, have our children profit from every experience life has to offer. We drive them to every lesson, enroll them in every sport. We think we are not doing enough for them, when actually we are stuffing so much into the day that by evening they—and we—are numb.

We must learn that "casual" has its place. Slowness is an art. Quiet and peace and solitude are desirable. Intensity only leads to exhaustion.

◆

The only way I can achieve peace is if I set my sights on it. I must learn to slow down, lessen the intensity of my life.

April 20

I don't know the key to success, but the key to failure is trying to please everybody.

—*Bill Cosby*

This is something we have a hard time remembering. As parents, we need to record these words and play them back throughout the day.

Perhaps your children ask a great deal of you. Your job has its own set of demands. Even if you could please everybody, would it be worth it? Would you derive a sense of satisfaction from giving everyone exactly what they want? Or would you feel used up—drained of all self-respect and sapped of all strength?

There is something to be said for your ability to say no. When you cannot, do not. You may displease some, but if they care for you enough, they will, in the end, admire your courage.

◆

I am no good to anyone if I say yes to everyone. Today I will remember that it is okay to say no.

Dear Mom and Dad: Leave $50,000 in a bag under
the bridge on Decatur Street. If there is no bridge on
Decatur Street, please build one.

—*Woody Allen*

One of the things we must learn to do as parents is to
say no to our children. They will beg, plead, cajole and
threaten. They will undermine our sense of confidence.
They will tell us we live on borrowed time. We must
remain strong.

Kids have a way of making us do things we would not
ordinarily do. We want to appear courageous. We want
them to think of us as invincible. They say, "Jump,"
and we hear ourselves answer, "How high?"

Obviously, this isn't advantageous—to them or us. If
we give our children everything they will have nothing
to fight for. If we make their lives too easy, they may
never be able to leave home.

◆

*I need to learn the difference between "raising" my children
and "accommodating" them.*

Don't think! Thinking is the enemy of creativity. It's self-conscious, and anything self-conscious is lousy. You can't try to do things; you simply must do them.
—*Ray Bradbury*

Give it a rest! To be a creative parent, let your mind relax. Thoughts will come more easily if you think less and enjoy it more.

We want our children to learn from us, so we may put too much energy into the process of parenting, instead of just allowing ourselves to "be" parents. When we "think" too much we are self-conscious and hardly at our best. Creativity has to flow unedited, as if channeled from the subconscious.

There is a connection we have to make—with ourselves—if we are to be effective parents. This connection has little to do with thought.

◆

I will try to "feel" my way through the day and see what It's like not to overprocess.

The trouble with the 1980s as compared with the 1970s is that teenagers no longer rebel and leave home.

—*Marion Smith*

Our teenagers aren't rebelling and leaving home— and, in some cases, neither are our thirty-year-olds. Are we making their lives too perfect, filled with every amenity? Are we making their homes too comfortable, a refuge from a less-than perfect world? Are we, in fact, aiding and abetting their escape from reality?

Our homes should mirror the outside world, so that our children, when the time comes, find comfort there. If we strive for perfection, it is likely that our children will be unable to live without it. Then, the world is likely to be a frightening place.

We want to make our children comfortable, but not so comfortable that the slightest difficulty makes them fly at top speed back to the nest.

◆

Nothing is more damaging to my children than the perfect world I have been trying to create for them. By letting them see reality "up close" I am giving them the confidence to explore it.

You gotta play the hand that's dealt you. There may be pain in that hand, but you play it.

—*James Brady*

We're never prepared for the "bolt from the blue." The unexpected storm that comes in the night. Life is about expecting the unexpected—not dreading it, but knowing that if it comes, you are prepared to meet it head on.

Parenthood is filled with promise, but it is not a panacea. We cannot rely on it to be trouble free—a cure-all for loneliness, an emotional release. We have children, and they may turn out to be the best thing that ever happened to us, but that does not mean there is no pain. We will be given our share of frantic days and sleepless nights. These go with the territory.

Whatever comes, we must prepare to face it. There are no guarantees. There is only hope.

◆

Anybody can make hay while the sun shines. I need to do my best while whistling in the dark.

If you've never been hated by your child, you've never been a parent.

—*Bette Davis*

Parenthood is not a popularity contest. There are days you'll be the most unpopular person on the block as far as your kids are concerned. As a parent, you need to expect this and to know that there's very little you can do about it.

Maybe what makes you an adult is the fact that you can stand up to it. You bend, but you don't break. You expect to be hated occasionally. You expect to be challenged. But if you play your cards right, you're always holding a royal flush. Your kids can yell and scream and slam the door, while you remain poised, your smile confident. You're a parent, and that's what you're here for after all.

Your kids may need you to be a sounding board, a punching bag, and a tower of strength. You need to stand still, sometimes, and be all these things.

◆

I don't always have to fight back. I understand that at times my kids need to challenge me and feel as if they've won.

April 26

He wants to live on through something—and in his case, his masterpiece is his son...all of us want that, and it gets more poignant as we get more anonymous in this world.

—*Arthur Miller*

If we expect to "live on" through our children, we are placing a terrible burden on them. They have to carry our expectations forward along with their own. Our ideas, our thoughts weigh heavily. They may be unable to discover and fulfill their own.

It's troublesome. We want to look at our nine-year-old without expectation. Yet we find ourselves expectant. We wonder if he will be a psychiatrist or a writer. We wonder if he will carry forward some of our dreams. We don't want him to be like us. We want him to be better.

We need to see that this is an encumbrance he does not need. If he can move freely in the world, without having to "live up" to our expectations, how much better off he will be.

◆

Expectations are a burden to my children. They'll do better if they can walk alone, without a lot of extra baggage.

There is always one moment in childhood that the door opens and lets the future in.

—*Graham Greene*

The future is right outside your front door. It's waiting to snatch your kids, when they're ready—to whisk them off to their destiny, while you wave goodbye.

This is your Faustian bargain. You get to keep them for eighteen years—and then they're off, to keep their appointment with fate. The control you thought you had over them never really existed. You were parenting on borrowed time. They knew this instinctively, but waited patiently for their moment.

When it's time to let the future in, don't fight it. The future is what you are working toward. It is giving you something to aim for, a gallery in which to exhibit your finest work.

◆

When it is time for my children to leave home, I will understand that this is the natural order of things, and let them keep their appointment with the future.

It is better to know some of the questions than all of the answers.

—*James Thurber*

Of course, Thurber is right. It is much, much better to question, to wonder than to know all of the answers. Where would be without our desire to learn, to go beyond the familiar?

But our children have so many questions, we may feel the need to answer them. We are, after all, supposed to be wiser than they are. If they look to us for guidance, for assurance, we're afraid we'll let them down if we admit we don't know.

The truth is, we do more for our children by encouraging their natural curiosity than by supplying them with the answers. Encourage the quest; don't solve it.

◆

To question is the natural right of my children. It may take a while for them to find all the answers.

There's nothing wrong with teenagers that reasoning with them won't aggravate.

—*Anonymous*

Trying to reason with your sixteen-year-old may be like trying to talk a cow out of standing on the railroad tracks. She doesn't care if the train is coming; she's found her place and she won't budge.

Still, you persist. Doing something, you think, has got to be better than doing nothing. Coaxing, pleading, offering explanations may produce results. So you think. But you're wrong. This is a case in which doing less may be doing more.

Your teenager needs your patience more than your reason.

◆

I will try to create a day without conflict—letting my teenager have some space and practicing patience.

April 30

The thing about having a baby is that thereafter you have it.

—*Jean Kerr*

There's no route back, no round-trip ticket. Once you're a parent, you're a parent for life. The infant in the next room who's crying for her bottle will some day expect you to give her away at her wedding. Kids don't come with money-back guarantees.

But remember, this works both ways: Your child can't trade you in either. She's stuck with the parents she gets. You and your child have struck a lifetime bargain and you both have to make of it the best that you can.

Maybe if you don't expect more of your children than they can give, they'll be satisfied with what you are able to give them in return.

◆

When I realize that my children are doing the best they can, I only feel compelled to do the best I can.

We learn geology the morning after the earthquake.
—*Ralph Waldo Emerson*

How often have we been too immersed in parenting to notice a shift in the emotional or physical landscapes of our children?

Parents who do too much sandbag the shore when the water is at neck level, because we tend, in the effort to parent effectively, not to notice nuance.

◆

I want to be more aware of the hints of problems ahead, but not to the extent that I create them.

M a y   2

If one talks to more than four people, it is an audience; and one cannot really think or exchange thoughts with an audience.

—*Anne Morrow Lindbergh*

When we need to get our parenting messages, directions, or opinions across quickly (and it's always quickly) we address our family members as though they were the first string of a basketball team.

If we want to have an interchange of ideas or opinions, we need to give our children the respect and time to react to us, most often privately.

◆

I do not want to be so pressed for time that I address the family as though they were members of a team, at half-time, in the locker room.

Zeal without knowledge is fire without light.
—*Samuel Butler*

When we buzz-saw through our days, parenting by the seat of our pants, being emphatic and breathless, we don't really give anything of ourselves. We are merely parroting yesterday's behaviors or what our parents may have inadvertently taught us.

And so there is no real warmth—even though we're throwing off a lot of heat.

◆

I know that I need to remind myself to be as present as I can be and not let my days with my children be vague and without heart.

M a y   4

The ant is knowing and wise; but he doesn't know enough to take a vacation.

—*Clarence Day*

Worker ants, that's what some of us have become. We've become indispensable, arrogant in the thought that we must forge ahead at all costs. And this nose-to-the-grindstone method of parenting gives us little or no time off.

A parent who is a study in constant motion is one who may be empty inside, pushing his task ahead, with no time off for good behavior.

◆

I shall be wise enough to know that I need time for myself, and time to enjoy those in whom I have invested so much.

Half our life is spent trying to find something to do with the time we have rushed through life trying to save.

—*Will Rogers*

Many of our parents, over and over again, have said "Time is so precious," or, "If I had it to do over again, I'd have started my family earlier, when I had the energy to raise the children in a better way."

Parents who do too much are always mindful of time. We try to economize time, attempt to manipulate the clock. Then, when we've rushed through our lives, and the early lives of our children, what do we have left? A clock staring at us, an empty house, and an empty heart.

◆

I know that one cannot "save" time. I want to take the time to be with my children, and absorb the joy they bring to me.

No one would have crossed the ocean if he could have gotten off the ship in the storm.

—*Anonymous*

When we are at wit's end, when our children have challenged us beyond all reason or imagination, when they disappoint us, and make us angry, we often think, "Why did we put him through school?" or, "What made me work two jobs to make certain she could take piano lessons?"

Well, here we are, in the middle of "parenting." We've certainly made a commitment to raise our children as best we can. But we should not think about abandoning what we've worked hard to create.

Those of us who are overcommitted parents need to remember our own childhoods and reflect on how our parents persevered, or better, stepped back, and allowed us to make our own mistakes.

◆

I need to think about how far we've come together, my children and I, how much we've learned and how much we have left to learn.

Some praise at morning what they blame at night,
But always think the last opinion right.
—*Alexander Pope*

Those of us who want the best for our children—the best schools, the best friends, the best clothes, the best sports, often lose sight of what our values really are.

If we listen to other parents who do too much, we may fall into the trap of not being consistent in our thoughts and our actions. We do not need to adopt the latest opinion or politically correct attitude we heard on television.

◆

It is confusing to our children when we overparent and change our minds and our opinions on what is important to their lives. Today is a day to reflect on how I can practice consistency.

Material abundance without character is the surest way to destruction.

—*Thomas Jefferson*

We need to discover ways in which we can help our children to discover their self-worth without giving them too many "things," and without overextending ourselves so that we do too much for them.

If our children are preoccupied with things we buy for them, then they cannot build character or a full personality; they will become dependent on the external and be people who do not know how to look within.

♦

I must understand that love, caring, and being listened to are the things my children most want, need, and crave.

Sadness hears the clock strike every hour. Happiness forgets the day or the month.

—*Seneca*

When we are at our best, we are not mindful of the clock or the calendar. It is only when we need time to rush by, to get us to a safe plateau, that we feel at ease.

Parenting is, as we know, a twenty-four-hour-a-day job. Even in our sleep, we remember our children. If we are not happy; if we do not find some degree of comfort in our role as guardians and teachers, then we are anonymous sentries who are meaningless to our children, and to ourselves.

◆

Today I let go. Today I roll around in the grass with my kids, or take them to a movie, or treat them and myself to an evening devoted to all of us.

The only way to get a serious message across is through comedy.

—*Woody Harrelson*

Maybe not the only way, but certainly one of the best ways. Allowing ourselves time to bring humor into our lives is very important. The job of parenting need not be grave, humorless, and cold.

If we try utilizing laughter as a means of getting a point across to our children, we will have made their day and ours all the brighter.

◆

When I want to get a point across to my children today, I will try to do it through laughter.

How do you know the fruit is ripe? Simple: When it leaves the branch.

—*André Gide*

Allowing our children to mature and ultimately become young adults and leave home is a terrifying thing for parents who do too much. We want to hold on to them, probe at them, keep them with us. After all, they have been the focus of our lives for seventeen or eighteen years.

We need to learn how to let go. If we do we may see that the fruits of our labor paid us handsomely: Our children have become healthy and happy adults.

◆

While I will not dwell on it, I do want to be aware that parenting is preparing my children to be balanced adults.

The greatest remedy for anger is delay.

—*Seneca*

When we are pushed to the wall by our children's un-controllable behavior, we need to remove ourselves mentally before we strike out in inappropriate and hurtful ways. Parents who do too much rarely have the time, real or imagined, to calmly and effectively deal with an insubordinate child. We too often lash out in-stantly, not allowing ourselves the time to think through our anger.

Doing too much can also mean acting too quickly. Peace may be restored, harmony achieved, if I think before I act.

◆

When I feel threatened by my anger, I will do my best to give myself time out to sort through my actions and their conse-quences.

Living at risk is jumping off a cliff and building your wings on the way down.

—*Ray Bradbury*

There is great risk in overseeing the development of any child. We tend to overparent if we try too hard to control.

So we must see that all of us are parenting without a net, and the risks we take can end up as rewards sometimes and mistakes other times. Parenting is, in many ways, like being an inventor—and every day we face risks and confrontations, but we never stop learning.

◆

We need to leave room in our lives to make mistakes, be more flexible, and not be afraid to invent parenting methods as we go.

Half our standards come from our first masters, and the other half from our first loves.

—*George Santayana*

We know we have an enormous impact on our children. They mimic our behaviors, our attitudes, our values.

What we need to remember is that imparting our beliefs is one thing—but attempting to instill them in our children is another. We should be aware that we are preparing them in many ways for their life partner and not raise limited, inflexible children.

If we give them the notion of "possibility," our children will be prepared for life and love.

◆

Today I will think about how I can help my children open up, seek answers and attitudes of their own. We will discover that they help shape their own standards.

The essence of being human is that one does not seek perfection.

—*George Orwell*

When we seek perfection, and most of us overcommitted parents do, we lose ourselves and our humanity, in the rush and rigidity of making things perfect. And perfection, in parenting, is a myth. There is no "one way" of bringing up children.

If we are so focused on the ways and means of rearing our kids, we cannot focus on who they are, or what they are becoming. In fact, it is our humanity, our kindness, openness and flexibility that children need.

◆

Today I will realize that perfection cannot be attained, because parenting is far from being an exact science.

Providing for one's family as a good husband and father is a watertight excuse for making money hand over fist. Greed may be a sin, exploitation of other people might look rather nasty, but who can blame a man for "doing the best" for his children?

—*Eva Figes*

All of us parents need to look at our own disease, namely workaholism and perfectionism, before we can clearly see how damaging to our families these sicknesses can be. Hiding behind work, disappearing in a cloud of commitments for the better good of our children is contradictory.

How many pairs of gym shoes do they need? How many tapes and CDs, designer jeans and stereos? What children really want is attention from their parents. They want to be able to trust them for their love and their openness. Things we provide for them are often the tangible results of overindulgence in the wrong way of "providing the best" for our children.

◆

If I am not cognizant of my own problems with being present and not losing myself in my work, I cannot be a sturdy and loving parent. I will think about this today.

When you are dealing with a child, keep your wits about you, and sit on the floor.

—*Austin O'Malley*

We often have trouble remembering our own childhood. The chances are good that we were "hurried" children, brought up by parents who were perfectionists in an imperfect atmosphere.

But it is very important to remember, as best we can, what it was like being a child. Only then can we effectively and appropriately enter the minds and hearts of our children, and not exact perfection from them.

◆

When we literally put ourselves on the same level as our young children, we are entering their world, and we will be welcome then, and in the future.

Children have to be educated, but they have also to be left to educate themselves.

—*Abbé Dimnet*

When we "overparent," we are too involved with virtually every facet of our children's lives. "Allowing" children to learn, to be educated is a gentler and far more appealing method of introducing them to life's studies.

Too much direction and monitoring smothers the curious child and sets the stage for a lifetime of mistrusting and shunning the process of education.

◆

Today I will stand back, and allow my children to self-direct their interests. It will be an adventure.

It takes all the running you can do, just to keep in the same place.

—*Lewis Carroll*

Haven't all of us felt this way? We work all day, come home to more work, and the trials of parenting, and we feel that we barely keep our heads above water.

Parents who do too much do run in place. For all of our activity, all the promises that must be met, and the impossible standards we've set for ourselves (and, often, for our children), we have only exhaustion and remorse to show for it.

◆

Today is a day to be reflective and idle. I refuse to get on my self-imposed treadmill.

Happiness sneaks in through a door you didn't know you left open.

—*John Barrymore*

Overcommitted parents are rarely, if ever, spontaneous. Instead, we plan our days and nights, and those of our children, with endless things to accomplish.

There's no room for chance, because everything is so overly orchestrated. To hear the song of a beautiful bird or notice the grace of a tree branch or the stillness of a pond in the hot noonday sun, you must be open to it.

We need to learn to allow ourselves to be happy. We often feel that parenting is a gruesome, exhausting job, and there is no room for spontaneity.

◆

Keeping an open door for surprise and to let fresh air into our lives is something I need to incorporate into every day.

The tongue is the deadliest of all blunt instruments.
—*Anonymous*

We often forget that brutality is not only enacted in a physical way. We find ourselves, at our overloaded worst, making snap decisions, bellowing orders, and belittling and shaming our children in the process.

Verbal violence is as abusive as physical violence. It may not leave a visible scar, but the child who is treated to derisive language will carry the results into his marriage and bequeath his damaged ego to his children.

When we are overburdened, it is the exact time to make certain that we do not take our frustrations and disappointments on the very people we are trying so hard to parent.

◆

I will be mindful of my anger and my tongue—I will not foist either on my children.

May 22

If you can't make it better, you can laugh at it.
—*Erma Bombeck*

When we're really in our disease we leave our humor behind. And when we can't change a little league baseball score, the results of a spelling test, or find all the Legos, we needn't take these things too seriously.

Parents who do too much often don't know how to laugh at themselves, because everything is serious, and anything that goes wrong is occasion for self-ridicule.

We need to get some distance on our lives. We need to realize those things that we can change for the better and those things we are powerless to change. Laughing may not be the remedy for everything, but it certainly lightens our load.

◆

Everything cannot be treated with the same amount of gravity. Today is a time to sort out what can be dealt with and what can be laughed off.

The teeth are smiling, but is the heart?
—*Congolese proverb*

How many times have we been shocked to find that a couple we know is filing for divorce? Or that there is alcoholism or drug addiction in a seemingly healthy family?

Those of us who would be perfect hide our pain and cover our losses by smiling through all of it, never admitting to ourselves, much less to others, that the burden of our perfectionism goes deep and leaves the heart spiritless and void of feeling.

Parents who do too much often spend too much time cosmetically hiding their pain.

◆

I want to be at one with what I really feel. I do not need to meet some ridiculously high standard I or others have set for me.

M a y   2 4

How often do we not see children ruined through the virtues, real or supposed, of their parents?
—*Samuel Butler*

One parent's virtue is another parent's vice.

Is it virtuous to have the children involved in baseball, soccer, the swim team, boy scouts or girl scouts, piano lessons, gymnastics, karate, voice lessons, and dance recitals? And is it virtuous for a parent to be scoutmaster, Sunday school teachers, chairperson of the school fund-raiser, president of the PTA, den mother, chauffeur, costume designer, seamstress, or all of the above?

Some of us will do everything and anything not to confront our loneliness and our problems.

◆

I want to focus on what I enjoy doing for my children and with my children. Filling up the calendar is not what I want for us.

Some defeats are more important than victories.
—*Michel de Montaigne*

It is foolish and destructive to think we must always "get our way" when we have a difference of opinion with our children.

"Giving in" on certain occasions or for various reasons allows our children to feel good about themselves and realize that they are not powerless and that we have respect for them.

The trick, of course, is to know on which confrontations you can give in. Instinctively, parents know what the really important issues are. What we need to remember is not to always control and "win over" our children.

◆

Giving in to get your way may sound manipulative, but it also may be good, kind parenting. I want to be more modulated in my "control" of my children.

In all our best efforts to provide "advantages" we have actually produced the busiest, most competitive, highly pressured and overorganized generation of youngsters in our history—and possibly the unhappiest.
—*Eda J. LeShan*

We want only the best for our kids. And only the best will do.

But what is the best? Parents who do too much very often have children who do too much. When the entire family is overextended and everyone has overachieved as best as he can, you have a house with the lights on, and nobody home.

A family that thrives on "activity" cannot hold together, nor can they expect the external to give them what they really need.

♦

I want my children to enjoy the feeling of being idle. Quiet reflection is rare, but we will make time for it.

Grownups never understand anything for themselves, and it is tiresome for children to be always and
forever explaining things to them.
                                —*Antoine de Saint-Exupéry*

Sometimes we don't listen to our children. When our
children are young, and do not employ self-censorship,
they have wonderful, direct, uncluttered things to say.

It is later, when we've force-fed them rules, manners,
and the tedium of life, that they begin to imitate us,
and be intimidated by our means and our methods.

◆

*I will listen to my young children. They can teach me so
much if I am willing to hear them.*

A man is not idle because he is absorbed in thought.
There is a visible labor and an invisible labor.

—*Victor Hugo*

Standing still, sitting quietly, or walking without purpose are all suspect activities. Parents who do too much
are usually a blur of activity. They don't have time for
introspection, nor do they trust such an idle and non-
productive activity.

And must we always be at labor? We know that we are
less productive, less accurate in our work when we go
overboard and hammer away without cessation. This,
of course, is a very dangerous thing to pass on to our
children. Dangerous and destructive.

◆

*I need to let my children see me busy at absolutely nothing.
I want them to build those times in their day.*

It is easy to live for others; everybody does. I call on you to live for yourselves.

—*Ralph Waldo Emerson*

Parents who do too much are often people completely and utterly bound up with their children. They live for them. And then, by no surprise, they begin to lose their own identity and merge their self-images into those of their children.

We need to know our own self-worth, who we are, and what makes us happy, contented, or feel whole. Absorption in our children and their lives is dangerous for both parties because it tyrannizes the child and makes a parasite of the parent.

◆

I want to see my children separate of me. I want them to be who they can be. I will work toward that end.

It costs more now to amuse a child than it used to cost to educate his father.

—*Anonymous*

Why do parents who do too much often find it necessary to make certain that their children are "amused" all the time?

Not only is the prospect of keeping a child "busy" expensive, it also takes an emotional toll on the parent and the child. And "things" are just that. Children who have too many "things" to amuse them will often find nothing within that will satisfy them. They will be left to seek external gratification, and will place little value on themselves or their abilities.

◆

Between the financial cost and the emotional price I pay, I know that when I am constantly trying to "amuse" my kids, I am caught in a dangerous trap.

Self-confidence is the first requisite to great under-takings.

—*Samuel Johnson*

If parents approach their children with insecurity, their children will become insecure. What we are is what we will undoubtedly pass along to the next generation.

If we begin each day with confidence, armed with the knowledge that our children learn more from who we are than from what we do, there is a great deal to gain.

The word "parent" is a label, applied to anyone who has a child. But we grow in this job. If we feel good about what we do, and not guilty about what we can-not do, we "become" parents. We may have much to learn, but we also have much to give.

◆

I will begin this day with the confidence to raise my chil-dren in the only way I can. I am competent in this job, even though I am learning daily.

J u n e   1

> The child had every toy his father wanted.
> —*Robert E. Whitten*

What happened to all the desires we had when we were children—the ones that went unfulfilled? Perhaps they are still with us, locked in our subconscious, only to resurface when we have our own children.

So we fill our children's playrooms with the toys we didn't get, their book shelves with the books we longed for. All the hopes and dreams of our youth have a second chance, the moment we have children. If we can give them all the things we were denied, maybe, in some small way, we will finally fill up the empty spaces.

We need to recognize that our children's needs are different from our own. Our children are not our second chance at life. They are their first chance at their own lives.

◆

If I fill up my children's lives with the things that are important to me, there may be no room left for the things that are important to them.

When I was a boy of fourteen, my father was so ignorant I could hardly stand to have the old man around. But when I got to be twenty-one, I was astonished at how much he had learned in seven years.
—*Mark Twain*

If you are constantly striving to impress your kids, showing them how much knowledge you have, how much prowess, how much courage, you will probably be disappointed. It's rare for kids to recognize such things in their parents, when they are, after all, trying to carve out a path for themselves.

As parents, we need to realize that our children will not always value the things we value in ourselves—but that someday, if we're fortunate, they may see us in a new light.

Kids are not kids forever. The child who challenges you today may be your closest friend in ten or fifteen years.

◆

If my kids don't praise me to the rafters, this doesn't mean I am not getting through to them.

" 'Tis by no means the least of life's rules to let things alone.

—*Baltasar Gracián*

Like an artist who admires his canvas—but thinks just one more brushstroke, and the work will be perfect—we find it hard to let our creations, our children, alone. We watch them, think about them, worry about them, analyze them. We are mystified when they do not seem to welcome this intrusion.

Our children may be our "creations," but their imperfections are what makes them human. Their weaknesses, their frailty, may be the spark that ignites them; their troubles are what they overcome in order to meet success. If we can never "let them alone," we may be robbing them of their chance for self-fulfillment.

◆

I will enable my children to ripen on the vine; they must be allowed to grow, blemishes and all, into mature adults.

Do not bind yourself to what you cannot do.
—*George Shelley*

There is an old saying: "Hitch your wagon to a star." True; but if the star is so high you cannot reach it, then what? If you overreach, if you try to grab hold of something that is unattainable, are you writing yourself a prescription for failure?

There are times we may wish we were magicians—that we could wave a magic wand and make everything perfect for our children. But attaching ourselves to this kind of fantasy is foolish.

Our children will find out that we are not superhuman. We cannot always make everything all right. But in accepting our own limitations they will also learn to accept their own.

◆

Knowing how to forgive myself may be the most important lesson I can pass on to my children.

Do not confuse your hunches with wishful thinking. This is the road to disaster.

—*Joyce Brothers*

Parents who do too much need to learn how to follow their hunches. Often, they are seeking help in many directions, afraid to look inward for answers.

We do, of course, have to learn the difference between following a hunch and wishing things to happen. One is instinct; the other is desire. What separates the two is thought. If you don't entirely trust your instincts it may be because you are trying too hard to control, to have it your own way.

A hunch is a purely instinctual response—based, of course, on past experience and even sound principle, but, nevertheless, coming straight from the heart.

◆

Parenting by instinct may be my best alternative. Today I will try not to overreason or overrationalize my responses.

Death and taxes and childbirth! There's never any convenient time for any of them.

—*Margaret Mitchell*

Trying to squeeze parenthood into an already busy life is a little like trying to stuff a full-grown elephant into a phone booth.

There is no convenient time to have children. Our lives will always be busy, stuffed with more things than we have time for, made miserable by constant demands, overburdened with all sorts of pressures—both external and self-imposed.

We "make room" for parenting by learning there are other things we can do without. As parents we lead different lives than the ones we led before, and we come to appreciate the value in our adaptability.

◆

There is no absolute cure for my busy schedule. I will learn to adapt my life, as needed, to the demands of being a full-time parent.

That's the part of it I [Sam Spade] always liked. He [Flitcraft] adjusted himself to beams falling, and then no more of them fell, and he adjusted himself to their not falling.

—*Dashiell Hammett*

Adjustment. This single word may sum up the kind of response parents, especially new parents, need to make. Every day, we are adjusting to new demands, new responsibilities, new expectations.

Just when we have our six-year-old figured out, he pulls something new from his bag of tricks, and we are called upon to make an adjustment. We are constantly having to adapt to the growth and change of our children, measuring our success by our ability to look at things from a new angle.

◆

My children need me to be tuned in. I will try to be more responsive, adapting to change as it happens.

Your mind must control, but you must have heart....Give your feeling free.

—*Vladimir Horowitz*

Most of us would like to set our feelings free. But to open up—to really give ourselves freely—is a frightening thing to do. When we get close to our feelings, we get close to pain. We admit that we are afraid of failure. We admit that the world is a scary place.

So we keep our feelings under control. We do not let our children see us as we really are. We let our minds rule, instead of our hearts. And, to avoid spending too much time with ourselves, we work ourselves to death. By overworking, overcompensating, overdoing, we prevent ourselves from getting close to our feelings.

But this is not living; this is self-imposed exile.

◆

If I can get closer to my feelings I can become a nurturing, supportive parent.

Happiness is equilibrium. Shift your weight. Equilibrium is pragmatic. You have to get everything into proportion. You compensate, rebalance yourself so that you maintain your angle to your world. When the world shifts, you shift.

—*Tom Stoppard*

That's it, then—all we need to know. When things go awry, it may be only the way we are looking at them. We need to reposition ourselves, view things from a different angle, and all will be right with the world.

Raising children is like being trapped in a hall of mirrors. It's hard to find your way through, because the mirrors fool you, continually changing your perception of reality. But think of Stoppard's words: When the scene shifts, you shift with it. When your children have new demands, new ideas, new personalities—when they force you to alter "reality"—you change, too.

◆

I will find "equilibrium" in parenting only when I realize that it changes daily. Today, listening to my children may help me regain my balance.

Be aware that a halo has to fall only a few inches to be a noose.

—*Dan McKinnon*

Being a parent does not make us angels. We don't have wings or a halo because we do too much. Doing too much is more reckless than selfless.

When we are overcommitted, we may tend to think of ourselves as larger than life, capable of everything and anything. But perfection is not the same as courage. Trying too hard and too much and too long is a trap, a noose around our necks. Suddenly, we are bound by our need for perfection. We can no longer forgive ourselves, or allow ourselves to rest.

If we are really interested in flights of mercy, we must begin with ourselves. By allowing ourselves the freedom to make mistakes, to come to the end of the line and begin again—this is how we earn our wings.

◆

Mistakes are opportunities. Today I will learn from my mistakes and go forward without self-punishment.

> You should treat all disasters as if they were trivialities but never treat a triviality as if it were a disaster.
> —*Quentin Crisp*

Parenting is not so much learning to take the good with the bad, as learning how to take the bad and make it seem less bad. There will always be those days—we've all had them—when everything seems to go wrong. To make those days bearable, we need to learn how to restore calm—and not to make "disasters" out of "trivialities."

Parents who do too much spend too much time in crisis. Our reactions are full-blown and dramatic, out of proportion to the event. We need to keep things in perspective. If our seventh-grader brings home a bad report card, it is not a disaster. If our sixteen-year-old stays out an hour too late, it is not a crisis. We are better parents if we don't panic.

By overreacting, we are contributing to the chaos. If we tone down our reactions to trivial things, we will also be able to handle the disasters when they come.

◆

I will try to be calmer today and see if it has a positive effect on those around me.

One should not be worried about the degree of "success" obtained by each and every effort, but only concentrate on maintaining the vision; keep it pure and steady.

—*Henry Miller*

Miller was talking about increments of success and how they lead to the "whole" of your life. You can be successful even if you have daily failures. You are leading toward something larger, more complete, than what you face each day.

It helps, as a busy parent, to understand that parenting is a process, and that no single "bad" day is a permanent blight on our record. If someone were keeping score, the good days and bad days would even out. And, in the end, we would see the beauty of the whole.

Parents who do too much are not keeping it "pure and steady." They are trying frantically to keep up with each day. The "whole" eludes them because they are too overcommitted to see it.

◆

Today I will try to keep it "pure and steady," understanding that the quality of the end product is more important than the sum of its parts.

June 13

The art of life is to know how to enjoy a little and to endure much.

—*William Hazlitt*

If we see ourselves as creators, perhaps we can identify with the artist who, having completed one quarter of his work, takes time to stand back and admire what he has done so far.

We can only benefit from our child-rearing responsibilities if we learn how to appreciate the results. If we take the afternoon off to spend time with our children, we not only get a much deserved rest—we also get to reap the dividends of our hard work.

◆

I can only give back what I am willing to receive. Taking time to enjoy the fruits of my labor will only increase my ability to give.

Whatever games are played with us, we must play no games with ourselves, but deal in our privacy with the last honesty and truth.

—*Ralph Waldo Emerson*

We are victimized by those we know best—our spouses, our friends, our children. They play mind games that we are drawn into—games that make us feel weak and powerless. It is difficult to put an end to these games even if we know they exist.

These games may ultimately wear us down. We forget what is real, what is honest. We allow ourselves to get caught up in other people's lies and deceptions. And, even in our most private moments, we forget how to be honest with ourselves.

As parents, we cannot afford to play games with our children. When we do this, we pass on harmful patterns of deceit and distrust.

◆

I need a few planned moments of introspection. I want to be totally honest with myself.

> Learn not to sweat the small stuff.
>
> *—Kenneth Greenspan*

There's a lot of "small stuff" that you can let go. Not every problem is a catastrophe; not every dilemma is a crisis. Parents who do too much tend to forget that some problems just go away on their own. We don't need to do something about everything that happens.

You have only to look back at yesterday to know that this is true. Can you even remember what your children were fighting about? Why you were so angry with your son?

Think of parenting as a magic slate. Every single day, you get a fresh start, a clean slate. The "small stuff" is wiped away and never comes back.

◆

Letting things go does not mean that I am incompetent or lazy. Sometimes, doing nothing is really the best thing I can do.

To grow, a lobster must shed its old shell numerous times. Each shedding renders the creature totally defenseless until the new shell forms…when risk becomes frightening, think of the lobster: vulnerability is the price of growth.

—*Richard Armstrong*

We wear our "busyness" like a suit of armor. When we have no schedule to hide behind, we risk letting our children and our spouses see us as we are—frightened, overwhelmed, out of control.

But growth requires exposure. Like the lobster who sheds his skin, we must be willing to let down our guard. We are our parents' children, after all, with all the fears, frustrations and illness they passed along to us. It is only when we face this truth that we can rise above it.

Putting too much on our plates may prevent us from noticing how little is left in our cupboards.

◆

I always thought it was important to have "something to do." Today I will see that my busy schedule is a subterfuge, preventing any chance of real growth.

The shoe that fits one person pinches another; there
is no recipe for living that suits all cases.

—*Carl Jung*

There is no "recipe for living" at all. What you've got
is a pinch of this, and a dash of that—an improvisa-
tional stew that may or may not taste just right.

Nor is there a recipe for successful parenting. You toss
together the ingredients at hand—some love, some
wisdom, some discipline—and you cross your fingers.
What works for you won't necessarily work for your
neighbor. Your kids are different; your personalities are
different; your lives are different.

You may wish your babies had been delivered with an
instruction booklet—that there was one good way to
do this—but, no. There are as many ways to parent as
there are parents.

◆

*I am someone's parent and this means having my own set of
standards and no one else's.*

Strange how much you've got to know before you know how little you know.

—*Anonymous*

Parenthood is humbling. No matter how much we do, sooner or later we realize how little we know. We may be here, there, and everywhere, but we can't find our way around the block. We may raise our son to the age of sixteen, but when he gets there, we may feel as if we know less than when we started.

Nothing we do in life requires this much humility. But, then, nothing we do in life offers us so much in return.

In the end, when our children are grown and no longer living in our homes, we will realize that what we learned is intangible. It is knowledge with no application, except to the spirit.

◆

What I am learning daily, as a parent, has little to do with changing the way I do things, but everything to do with changing who I am.

People become house builders through building houses, harp players through playing the harp. We grow to be just by doing things which are just.

—*Aristotle*

The great philosopher understood the wisdom of learning by doing. Accomplishment is born out of undertaking. What we do is what we become. As we parent, we become parents.

If we accept that this is true, perhaps we will have less to prove. We will understand that everyday is a learning experience, a part of the process of "becoming." We cannot expect ourselves to be wiser or stronger or more capable than we are. We can only expect ourselves to handle each experience as it occurs.

When it is all over, we who "parent" daily—we who have been entrusted with the lives of children—will have "become" parents.

◆

I am in the process of becoming a parent. What I do daily is what I will become.

No answer is also an answer.

—German proverb

We do not always "owe" our children an answer.

Parents who do too much feel "responsible" to their children every moment of the day. But our children do not need a commitment on every issue, an answer to every question at the moment it is asked.

If we are always on call for our children, we are cheating ourselves out of the right to remain silent. We cannot give our children what we do not have to give. When we are tired, when it is late, when the well is dried up, we must learn that it is okay not to have an answer, and that no answer might be better than some response we make in haste.

◆

I need to let my children know when I have nothing worthwhile to say or nothing left to give.

June 21

Let your children go if you want to keep them.
—*Malcolm Forbes*

We have learned about boundaries. In parenting, too, there are lines we may not cross. We may think that the babies we hold and bathe and feed and diaper "belong" to us. We must not confuse "love" with "ownership." Our children are separate beings, and no matter what we do for them, we have our own lives—and they theirs.

If we are holding them too close, trying too hard to keep them with us, it is because we are protecting ourselves from a life without them. But sooner, rather than later, we must learn to let go. If nothing else, history has shown us that "control" breeds rebellion, and, ultimately, separation. If we try to imprison them, we will undoubtedly lose them.

◆

In doing too much for my children, I may be pushing them away. Today I will try to recognize their need for a separate identity, respecting their right to independence.

We can have a surfeit of treasures—an excess of shells, where one or two would be significant.
—*Anne Morrow Lindbergh*

How can we know what is really important to us—how can we hope to separate the important from the trivial—when our lives are so full?

On an island, with little to do, Lindbergh was able to see the importance of the few available things: the "gifts from the sea." But in our busy lives, with so much that we are responsible for, so many things to fill our calendars, how can we separate the important from the trivial? How can we find our one or two shells that are significant?

When our calendars are full, it is likely that our hearts and minds are also full; even our children, whom we love, are taken for granted. To see their importance, to recognize the wealth of riches that are all around us, we may need to give ourselves more space, more time to be alone.

◆

If I spend some time alone I may be able to discover treasures that were always there.

Some of us are ground crew—holding lines, building fires, dreaming dreams, letting go, watching the upward flight. Others of us are bound for the sky and the far edges of things.

—*Robert Fulghum*

All of us are different, with different styles and a different life purpose. We bring these differences to our children.

Some of us are "ground crew," giving our children a strong foundation to build on. We are the ones who do what needs to be done, teaching our children the rewards of good work, the pleasures to be found in seeing things through.

Others are dreamers, visionaries. We may encourage our children to see not only the possible, but the impossible. We show them how far we have come, and encourage them to go further still, building their own dreams, creating their own challenges.

◆

I cannot expect myself to be "all things" to my children. There are many people they will learn from—all with important contributions to their growth.

We must confront, in the dreams we dream, as well as our intimate relationships, all that we never will have and never will be.

—*Judith Viorst*

As parents, we can dream; but we must also face reality: No matter how much we do for our children, they will never be everything we wish them to be.

Perhaps we think that if we are good parents, if we always expect the best from our children, we can help them overcome their limitations. But we need to face reality. Our children may never be the doctors or lawyers or physicists or long-distance runners we wish them to be. They may never be able to live up to the goals we set for them. And, knowing this, knowing they may disappoint us, they may grow away from us, preferring the company of friends who demand less of them.

◆

I will do a daily reality check to make sure I am not allowing my dreams for my children to interfere with their well-being. I do not want to frighten them away.

Parents: A peculiar group who first try to get their children to walk and talk, and then try to get them to sit down and shut up.
—*Wagster's Dictionary of Humor and Wit*

It's tiring just to think about it! First we waited impatiently for the first steps; then we listened intently for the first word. We cooed and coaxed and bragged to our neighbors. We took photographs and videos to record those magical moments.

Then, not more than a few weeks later, we were using the same energy (or what was left of it) to beg them to stop. Suddenly, that baby that looked so cute in the cradle was emptying drawers, banging pots and pans—still brilliant, of course, but oh so uncontrollable. So we spent even more energy trying (in vain, of course) to get her to stop, to sit down, to calm down.

These turnabouts of parenting are unavoidable; still, if we think about how quickly things change, we may learn not to be overly invested in the present.

◆

Although each stage of my child's growth is important, I will try to save enough energy for the next stage to come.

One never notices what has been done; one can only see what remains to be done.

—*Marie Curie*

Parents need to take stock occasionally. It's great to have goals; but when we reach them, we need to acknowledge it. Instead of regarding our three-year-old as an unfinished adult, we should try to see him as a complete and healthy three-year-old who's doing just fine. For this, we deserve to take credit—and certainly to have some sense of pride.

There are many hills to climb before we reach the top of the mountain. We need to take some time, on top of each hill, to look around and enjoy the view.

◆

I owe it to myself to find time for self-congratulation.

The trouble with being in the rat race is that even if you win you're still a rat.

—*Lily Tomlin*

The truth is, you may get what you want, but you might not like what you've turned into, once you get it.

To offer your children "the most" and "the best" you may have to rush through your life, making demands on others, expecting them to step aside for you. You'll encounter your share of roadblocks, and you'll need to lie or cheat or bully your way through them. If you are handling two or three jobs, you may turn into the kind of monster your children won't want to face when you finally do come home.

You may think it is impossible to do it any other way. After all, it's a jungle out there. You're only doing what you think you must do so that your children get enough. But what is enough? Is it possible that you— and your children—could get by with less?

◆

I may be able to do more for my children by doing less. I say I am "doing it all for them," but I have given too much of myself away.

It is hard to fight an enemy who has outposts in your head.

—*Sally Kempton*

The enemy is close at hand; he is us. When we spend our days, frantically trying to absorb all that we can, be all that we can, do all that we can, we are our own worst enemies. We may blame the clock. The truth is that we are the generals of this war, and we wage it daily against ourselves.

The battle scars are deep. There is no way to keep up with the impossible demands we place on ourselves. From the moment we wake up in the morning, that little voice is going off in our heads: Do more, earn more, be more, give more.

We need to fight back with all our strength. We can defeat this villain who has set out to destroy us. We can defeat him because we know him well.

◆

I am my own worst enemy when I am living with this disease called workaholism.

If you want a baby, have a new one. Don't baby the old one.

—*Jessamyn West*

Babies are helpless and adorable and need our full attention. Ten-year-olds do not. Every day we need to modify our roles as parents, because our children have grown and changed and no longer need the same things from us. What we gave to our toddler, we cannot and should not give to our teenager.

Perhaps, when our children need less of our time and energy, that is the time to redirect ourselves. Otherwise, we are in danger of overparenting—of "babying" our children long after they need it.

Parents who do too much often don't know when it is appropriate to "stop" doing. Long after it is necessary, they are still spoon-feeding.

◆

I need to think about how I'm spending my energy. I may be overdoing it, especially in relation to my older children.

The first problem for all of us, men and women, is not to learn but to unlearn.

—*Gloria Steinem*

We are practiced in the art of fooling ourselves, acting in our own worst interests. At our overcommitted best, we have nothing to offer ourselves or our children. We want to change. But how do we do it?

Some of what we do we have done for years, having watched our parents—who watched their parents— who watched theirs. It may take daily practice to go up against the legacy of generations.

But we can change if that is what we really want. We can be better, calmer, less harried parents, if that is what we choose to be.

◆

I am confident that I can tear down the structure of old patterns and set a better example for my children.

July 1

Do everything right, all the time, and the child will prosper. It's as simple as that, except for fate, luck, heredity, chance, and the astrological sign under which the child was born, his order of birth, his first encounter with evil, the girl who jilts him in spite of her excellent qualities, the war that is being fought when he is a young man, the drugs he may try once or too many times, the friends he makes, how he scores on tests, how well he endures kidding about his shortcomings, how ambitious he becomes, how far he falls behind, circumstantial evidence, ironic perspective, danger when it's least expected, difficulty in triumphing over circumstance, people with hidden agendas, and animals with rabies.

—*Ann Beattie*

Even for us parents who do too much, it is clear we cannot control the earth, its people, and the stars above.

◆

I must realize that each day I must let there be enough of myself intact so that my investment in my children does not bring on my emotional bankruptcy.

The thing to do is supply light and not heat.
—*Woodrow Wilson*

We have seen many parents who, whether in casual circumstances or in more formal settings, cannot leave their children alone. They are all over them, concerned about every breath they take. Even their "adult" conversation centers around their children almost exclusively. They plan each day, each hour for their kids until both parent and child are exhausted by schedules, calendars and events.

When we hover over our children, we cast *our* shadows—and do not allow the light to fall on our children, squelching growth, and hampering development.

◆

If we create an environment for our children where they feel safe to learn, to stretch, to explore on their own, we will have given them a special gift.

July 3

Martyrdom has always been proof of intensity, never the correctness of a belief.

—*Albert Schweitzer*

Parents who do too much are often very intense, too highly focused in their parenting. When the inevitable happens, that of a child's failure to live up to our Matterhorn-sized expectations, a curious thing happens. We become martyrs—suffering through our children's childhood as though it were a test of *our* endurance.

We need to step back and reevaluate our lives and our expectations. Are we trying to live our children's lives for them, or are we allowing ourselves and our children to make mistakes and learn their own life lessons?

◆

When I begin to feel the martyrdom coming on, I will step back, and take a look at the source of my unhappiness.

To do nothing is the most difficult thing in the world—the most difficult and the most intellectual.
—*Oscar Wilde*

Certainly we're not talking about watching idly while our children get involved in terrible problems like drugs and alcohol or casual sex.

There are, though, some experiences that our children need to have in order for them to become self-sufficient young adults and adults with character.

We must steel ourselves when our daughter comes home brokenhearted because her boyfriend dated her best friend—we cannot adopt and thereby dispense with her pain. And when our son comes home not having been chosen for the soccer team, we cannot stand in for him and erase his humiliation.

◆

Without inflicting pain, sometimes we must allow our children to experience their own pain—in their own way.

July 5

> We cannot carry our father's corpse with us every-
> where we go.
>
> —*Guillaume Apollinaire*

Our parents had an astounding effect on our lives, and
that is how it should be. But what happens to us, as we
grow into adulthood, shackled to their ways and methods of parenting—their opinions? Often what we
learned from our parents does not apply to raising children in our world.

Outmoded, inflexible, and sometimes damaging dem-
agoguery often surfaces when we begin to rear our own
kids.

◆

*We need to question what we learned as children from our
parents, and be careful not to repeat the traits we felt were
damaging to us.*

But I think parents aren't teachers anymore. Parents—or a whole lot of us, at least—lead by mouth instead of by example.

—*Robert R. McCammon*

In this very crazed, seat-of-the-pants way in which we're forced to parent these days, we all too often forget to show rather than to tell.

A set of rules rattled off over breakfast and a recap of duties reeled off over dinner does not bring the family closer together or leave the children with values or insights. Instead, it takes away the human touch, the need for children to see a moral lesson in process, or learn grace through close-up observation of their parents.

◆

We need to stop believing that everything our children need to learn can be and is being taught at school. The fundamental, most long-lasting lessons our children learn are acted out at home.

You must be willing to bend; you can't allow your-self to think for one moment that you are a "prisoner" of your "ideas."

—*Will Steger*

Virtually every day, when we roll out of bed, we have a set of ideas, thoughts, appointments that we intend to rigorously fulfill.

And as we move through the day, we are confronted perhaps hundreds of times by people who question our judgments and our conclusions.

While we should not be so flexible that we haven't any consistent strength of character, we need to be open enough to the possibility of change, of the right to question our opinions.

◆

If we become hostage to a set of beliefs and act on them rigidly and religiously, we will bring up our children to be inflexible, unhappy, and close-minded adults.

Kirk was never afraid to come down pretty hard when we deserved it. Sometimes divorced parents have this guilt, and so they always give in to the kids. He used to say, "I yell and scream because I care."

—*Michael Douglas*

Parents who do too much are often, especially in the case of separation or divorce, supersensitive to their children. They may overparent because they feel they've failed their children and want to make it up to them.

It's important that we understand overindulging our children may hurt them. Children, especially children of divorce, need their parents to act honestly. If what they feel is betrayal, the last thing they need is overindulgence.

It is important to understand that parenting is not a popularity contest. Whether we yell and scream or speak in whispers, we need to be saying what they need to hear.

◆

I do not want to focus on my guilt for having failed. I want to focus on how I can make a success of creating a life-long, life-fulfilling relationship with my children.

A mother is not a person to lean on, but a person to make leaning unnecessary.

—*Dorothy Canfield Fisher*

When our children are very young, they obviously "lean" on us for their needs. As they grow into school-aged kids, they learn to be independent. We can help them on the road to independence by allowing them to feel capable of making decisions—even simple ones—as soon as they are ready.

It is often difficult to gauge this "readiness" because so many of us want to keep our children dependent. We erroneously believe that if they always "need" us we may always hold on to them.

But when does the "need" stop? Do we want our children to grow into "needy" adults? Are these the kind of people we choose as friends? Keeping our children dependent is a risky game—a dangerous high-wire act that always ends up in failure.

◆

Independence and self-reliance are the two things we must instill in our children. Otherwise, they may be terrified to grow up and leave the nest.

We pardon to the extent that we love.
—*La Rochefoucauld*

We've all heard the phrase before, and maybe some of try to practice its message: unconditional love.

If our children act out (as all children do), talk back, fight, and generally disappoint us, we need to remember that these behaviors are, to a certain extent, all part of growing up.

If we love our children and are deeply committed to them, we sometimes confuse "control" for "nurturing." And when we pardon ourselves for being "human" instead of always being "humane," we then begin to understand that our love is directly proportionate to our capacity to forgive.

◆

When we have unencumbered love for our children, we are partners in the process, not tyrants.

July 11

The average, healthy, well-adjusted adult gets up at seven-thirty in the morning feeling just plain terrible.
—*Jean Kerr*

Most of us do wake up exhausted. Since we've crammed so much into the day and evening before, we've really not given ourselves enough rest when it's time to jump back into the fray.

When we take care of ourselves, get enough sleep, eat the right kind of healthy foods, get some exercise, and build in time for fun each day, we not only take care of ourselves—we are creating an environment that helps us take care of our children.

◆

There is a kind of ecology of the family. If one member suffers, or is unhappy, it affects the entire family. The whole of the family is not necessarily greater than its parts. We are interdependent and our ecology needs to be in balance.

Nothing is more sad than the death of an illusion.
—*Arthur Koestler*

Parents who do too much always seem to be superhuman—or not human at all.

As children we did not see our parents for what they were—just people, trying more often than not to do the right thing.

The illusion of our parents as being above human frailty, without human traits and faults, is a myth that is dangerous and keeps us at arm's length emotionally from our children. It is important, and perhaps somewhat painful, for our children to see us as "people," not perfect and not infallible.

◆

In order for my children not to put me on a pedestal, I may need to remind them that all of us are more alike than unalike.

July 13

The worst misfortune that can happen to an ordinary man is to have an extraordinary father.
—*Austin O'Malley*

Or mother.

In our drive to become "extraordinary" people with "exemplary" children, we often become overachievers, and the crazy standards we set for ourselves are transferred to our children.

When we do this, when we expect our children to "measure up" to the goals we have set for ourselves, we do not take their individuality into account. Too often, we see them as mere extensions, assuming that they, like us, will be the best at everything they undertake.

◆

Deep footsteps left by an overachieving mother or father are often never filled by their children. We need to remember not to compete with our children or become symbols of unattainable stature.

An appeaser is one who feeds a crocodile hoping it will eat him last.

—*Winston Churchill*

When we attempt to appease our children, cushioning every unpleasant thing that may come their way, and warding off all demons, real or imagined, we are creating monsters.

Parents who do too much often protect too much. We can, without realizing it, make our children into people who are never prepared for failure, loss, or disappointment.

Sooner or later, it's the parent who's eaten by the crocodile—because we've failed to allow our children to feel pain. And they will resent us for it.

◆

I want my children to be happy, but I want them to be prepared for failure. I must occasionally look away when they are in the path of oncoming adversity.

July 15

The more corrupt the state, the more numerous the laws.

—*Tacitus*

Parents who do too much often create a police state in the home. There are so many rules to follow, regulations to be aware of, schedules to adhere to, and no variances tolerated.

When we create this atmosphere, we engender a climate with no flexibility, one where anger and resentment run rampant. We hide our insecurities about parenting behind a plethora of unwavering statutes.

◆

If life is about growth, change, and spirituality, I will do my best to create an environment where those things can flourish. Although I know some "house rules" must be established, I will not create a prison with rigid regulations.

Most times, after my mother made dinner, my father would put the apron on and do the dishes, and that was never beneath him . . . . . It didn't even occur to him that it might make him look wimpy or henpecked. I definitely picked up that attitude from my dad. And the way I've used it in my own life is by treating women, men, and children—with respect.

—*Robert Pastorelli*

When our children see that families—and marriages—can be equal partnerships, without gender-specific tasks adhered to, they will undoubtedly be more open, more hospitable to that kind of life. Young boys and girls who see their parents working in harmony, not driven by tradition or role playing, will be better parents.

◆

I want my children to learn how a home can be a safe place for everyone, a place where cooperation wins out over ego.

Make three correct guesses consecutively, and you will establish a reputation as an expert.

—*Laurence Peter*

Deep down, we know that parenting is at least 50 percent guesswork. Trusting ourselves, our powers of reasoning and logic does not come easily for parents who do too much.

We consult book after book on child rearing, certain that we're incapable of making the "right" decision.

Only when we begin to relax, and actually enjoy the process of parenting, will we allow ourselves to depend on our instincts, and not question every interaction we have with our children.

◆

I cannot depend exclusively on "outside" information. I will begin looking within for guidance, and learn how to trust myself in the process.

Silence is one of the great arts of conversation.
—*Anonymous*

Many of us talk almost incessantly. We're not only busy running all over town, from one meeting to the next, chauffeuring the kids from one volleyball game to the next swimming lesson, we're usually chattering away the entire time.

Everyone knows that when one is talking one is not listening. We do not indulge our child by listening to him. Listening to other persons not only sheds light on their life and their experiences; it is also an act of kindness, both for the listener and the speaker.

◆

I want to establish a genuine communication between me and my children. If I cannot listen, I cannot give.

Never fear spoiling children by making them happy. Happiness is the atmosphere in which all good affections grow.

—*Ann Eliza Bray*

Creating a happy environment should not be work. Parents can find small ways to create an atmosphere that is bright, open, and cheerful.

We need not buy them the latest toys, the most expensive bikes, or build a tennis court in the backyard. Being inventive, and joining in the fun will create children who will know how to pass this spirit along to their children.

◆

A house where there is joy and laughter is a gift, and one that gives back a hundredfold. I want that kind of environment for my family.

Loving is not just looking at each other, it's looking in the same direction.

—*Antoine de St. Exupéry*

Parents who do too much are often at odds with each other. It may never be intentional, but nonetheless a mother and father may be traveling at breakneck speed in opposite directions.

Parents who do not have a common goal for their children or an agreement on how to attain it may love their children, but they are doing them a major disservice.

Harmony of philosophy, of goal, of means to an end, bespeaks love that is directed from the heart and the head.

◆

When there is commonality of thought, there can be magnificent results. I will work with my spouse to create a united, loving, and supportive atmosphere for our children.

The worst pain we can have is to know much and be impotent to act.

—*Herodotus*

Parents who do too much find themselves in this situation often. We want desperately to control our children's lives, choose the "right" friends, make certain they get the "best" teachers.

But although it may be a cliché, it is nonetheless true: Experience is the best teacher. By planning our children's lives, we rob them of the right to grow into certain experiences for themselves.

We have years of experience and knowledge beyond theirs, and so we see things they could not possibly see. Still, we cannot use this powerful insight every single time we have it. It is often painful to see our children hurt, frightened, or about to fail. But certain life lessons have to be learned, not taught, and—most definitely—not avoided.

◆

There are times to step in and save our children from pain. There are times when they must endure the pain in order to grow. I hope I can be wise enough to know the difference.

The fundamental defect of fathers is that they want their children to be a credit to them.

—*Bertrand Russell*

We cannot shape our children in our image, or one we find even more attractive. Children are not topiary, and they will not grow as their genetic code dictates; instead, they will reflect in their behavior the way they have been treated.

If we really want our children to "be a credit" to us, we ought to think less in terms of their goals and more in terms of their values. It matters less that they turn into "the architect," "the banker," or "the gold-medal athlete" and more that they lead happy, decent lives as healthy, responsible adults.

◆

My children don't owe me a successful life; they owe themselves a chance at life.

The aim of an argument or discussion should not be victory, but progress.

—*Joseph Joubert*

Parents who do too much are often people who argue too much, and feel the need to "win" every argument they have.

Confrontation, disagreement, differences in style and taste always surface in any family. But we must be aware that we are all entitled to our views, and that, in most matters, there cannot be a "winner."

If we can exorcise our egos from a disagreement, not worry about who can best prove a point, and stop acting as if the family were two debating teams—the kids against the adults—then we will learn from our differences.

◆

Even if I feel my child may be terribly misguided or have inadequate information, it is still important that I hear his views. Only then will I know how best to parent.

Weird clothing is de rigueur for teenagers, but today's generation of teens is finding it difficult to be sufficiently weird...because the previous generation, who went through adolescence in the sixties and seventies, used up practically all the available weirdness.

—*P. J. O'Rourke*

Remember bell-bottoms and tank tops? Wide belts and see-through shirts? Hot pants and clogs? Or maybe for you it was poodle skirts, anklets, and bobby sox—or T-shirts with the sleeves rolled up and pointed black boots.

Today it may be dreadlocks and brushcuts, bandanas and cowboy boots, but each generation creates its own look, its own identity, and most of it shouldn't be taken too seriously.

◆

If my children go through adolescence in the fashion of their day, I will do my best to allow them to express themselves. I will, however, draw the line at allowing them to insert safety pins and other hardware through their noses.

Mental reflection is so much more interesting than TV, it's a shame more people don't switch over to it.
—*Robert M. Pirsig*

Our generation, the ones who are now struggling with parenting, grew up during the birth of the information society, which has now become the society aglut with information.

When TV was born it was a seemingly benign appliance, one that gave us a few laughs and not much of anything else. Now it is a giant, dispensing information from an amazing number of channels, and in no small way is it responsible for parenting on the fast track. Now we get twenty-four-hour news, weather, sports, and MTV. We have to keep up with our kids who are also getting their share of information—from "Sesame Street," "Kids News" programs, "Mr. Wizard," and "The Simpsons."

It is not by accident that we do not go within—we live our lives externally, searching only for the stimulation that contradicts self-exploration.

◆

What we can learn from ourselves by looking within is most likely more worthwhile than anything we can tune in to.

The more you love your children, the more care you should take to neglect them occasionally. The web of affection can be drawn too tight.

—*D. Sutten*

We've all seen children being "loved to death." Parents who are incessantly hugging and cooing over their offspring may be overcompensating for feelings of self-doubt or insecurity—or, perhaps, for having felt unloved as children.

The act of suffocating a child with love is a debilitating (for both parents and child) and intrusive act. Instead of building confidence and trust in a child, this kind of parenting tends to make the child fearful, detached, and, ironically, incapable of any depth of emotion.

◆

An overabundance of anything can cause great distress; even with the best of intentions, I will not initiate a cycle of neediness in my child.

I do not want to build my life around you, but I do want to include you in the building of my life.
> —*Harold Bloomfield, Melba Cosgrove,*
> *and Peter McWilliams*

Overcommitted parents are almost always totally committed to their children. Our world begins and ends with our kids; we pin all our hopes on them, attempt to make their environment perfect in every way.

We can live together, and not at one another's expense, with mutual love and respect. Our voices should be heard separately and together. Our children are so very important to us. But if they become our sole interest, it is the beginning of the loss of the self.

◆

I want to co-exist with my children. I do not want to lose myself in their lives.

I can govern the United States, or I can govern my daughter Alice, but I can't do both.

—*Theodore Roosevelt*

President Roosevelt had his hands full. His daughter, who later became one of the most controversial, witty, and famous women of Washington ("If you have nothing nice to say, come sit by me.") was terrifically outspoken and full of fire.

Obviously, his statement was meant to be funny, but there's more than a grain of truth in it.

Our jobs and careers can overwhelm us; we find it so difficult to juggle the rearing of our children with the time we need to devote to our work. Overwhelmed: the one-word definition of a parent who does too much.

◆

I must be aware of my limitations. They are as important to acknowledge as my strengths.

Tact is the intelligence of the heart.

—*Anonymous*

When we're in a rush (and when are we not?) we tend to "cut to the chase," speaking to our children and our spouses quickly, without thinking first. Sometimes what we say can be hurtful, even if unintentionally so.

Tact is important when we're introducing a subject our children may be sensitive about. And timing is as important as tact.

We need to treat our children as humans; not as defective adults who are resilient enough to bounce back from an inadvertent—and tactless—remark.

◆

I want to be kind and to engender kindness. I want to be tactful when speaking to my children.

Say not "I have found the truth," but rather "I have found *a* truth."

—*Kahlil Gibran*

Life is rarely about absolutes. Life is more about shades of gray than it is about black and white.

Overcommitted parents often deal in absolutes. Our certainties are our life preservers. We want to believe that there is a right way and a wrong way, without nuance or gradation.

All of us have separate truths. The soup that is too spicy for you is perfect for me. What appears to be a rose to me may be a stem of thorns to you.

◆

In our need to be certain, we rush too often to judgment. I want to be more open to the different realities within my family unit.

The most important thing a father can do for his children is to love their mother.

—*Theodore M. Hesburgh*

When we demonstrate love, through words, physical gestures, smiles—hands clasped as we enjoy a walk with the family—it speaks volumes to our children.

Our kids are perceptive. They don't need to be hit over the head with demonstrations of love. But a harsh word, spoken in haste, may lead to a full-blown argument—the kind that makes a child frightened that he may lose his family. At these times, a child feels alone and powerless.

We cannot provide an environment that is free of discord; but we must be aware that the children who see and hear love demonstrated are the ones who feel most secure.

◆

I will be more mindful to show affection and warmth to my spouse. Our children will be the beneficiaries.

Learn the wisdom of compromise, for it is better to bend a little than to break.

—*Jane Wells*

In business, we understand this principle. In friendship, we understand it. But, for some reason, we have a hard time applying it to our children.

Yet, time and again it has been proven: Compromise works. If we offer our kids an alternative solution, instead of giving them an unresilient, unwavering "no," we're bound to come to a meeting of the minds. Our kids will appreciate the fact that we respect their opinions and may "bend" a lot quicker than we think.

Otherwise, we're seen as the enemy. And why not? After all, we have all the power, all the control, all the resources—*and* a secret plan of attack. We certainly *seem* like the aggressor.

◆

I will not encourage my children to see me as "the enemy." I can keep the spirit of compromise alive in our family—and still maintain my authority.

Life forms illogical patterns. It is haphazard and full of beauties which I try to catch as they fly by, for who knows whether any of them will ever return?
—*Margot Fonteyn*

To see the beauty of life, one has only to look around. Beauty, in its own random way, is all around us: in the falling of the leaves; in the grace of a swan; in the tiny hands of our children.

We must understand that as these things "pass by," it will probably be for the last time. Nature recycles itself; seasons change; children grow into adults, then have children of their own. To reach out and seize the moment, we have to understand its uniqueness. If we do not notice it, if we do not make time for it, the moment passes, never to come again.

This is our chance to be parents. This is our one and only chance.

◆

The moment exists only if I reach out and take notice of it. Today I will try to spend a moment with my children, conscious that in grabbing hold of the present, I am making a commitment to the future.

The worst waste of breath, next to playing a saxophone, is advising a son.

—*Kin Hubbard*

The president has advisers. Children don't need them. Children have parents who "pretend" to be advisers, and children "pretend" to listen. The truth is, the only advice children are willing to listen to is the advice they give themselves.

If you want to give advice to your kids, save your breath. Talk to your kids instead. Talk to them about baseball and horses and politics and weather and the price of fame. Talk to them about animals and presidents and music and the time you had the time of your life. Give them encouragement and praise and warmth and wit. Anything but advice.

◆

Those who give advice may have to open themselves up to receive it. I prefer an open exchange of ideas without the encumbrance of ego.

A food is not necessarily essential just because your child hates it.

—*Katherine Whitehorn*

Oh, but the myriad of ways we use to cook broccoli! Chop it up and place it in the hamburger (they'll never suspect); process it into a fine paste and spread it on crackers; boil it into a delicious soup. We've got to get those kids to eat their broccoli!

Do we? Will they grow up into unruly, unfeeling, unsatisfied adults if they never eat broccoli?

Parents who do too much often act like slaves in the kitchen, trapped by their belief that kids "need" certain foods, even if they don't want them. In fact, sometimes it's the foods they don't want that become an issue. We wage war in the kitchen, armed with our pots and pans, ready to do battle.

◆

Food issues are not only harmful to my children, they create battle zones. If my child is healthy, he can live without a couple of foods he dislikes.

Action should culminate in wisdom.

—*Bhagavad Gita*

What it boils down to is this: What we "do" ought to amount to something. When we run helter-skelter, in the frantic activity of our daily lives, we're not "doing" something in the real sense. This kind of frenzied activity serves no moral purpose; nor does it make us wiser. This kind of "doing" just gets things done.

Real action is born of enthusiasm and drive, courage and ambition. When we are active in this way, we promote ourselves, and further our lifelong goals. Too often, parenting requires the "other" kind of action, draining us of our energy and leaving us exhausted.

We need to give ourselves enough time for "real" action, real purpose in our lives. Whether it be dedication to a cause, spending creative time with our children, devotion to our religion, or furthering our education, we need to follow some activity that "culminates in wisdom."

◆

To be fully alive I need to take advantage of what life can offer me. If I am spending my days in frantic pursuit of "getting things done," I may be missing my true purpose.

People love chopping wood. In this activity one immediately sees results.

—*Albert Einstein*

Parenting is the opposite; the results are far down the road. Daily, we put ourselves into the task of parenting, and daily, we wonder if our efforts are worthwhile. Children grow ever so slowly—the change in them as imperceptible as the breeze.

Still, even without tangible results, we can feel good about the work we do. The woodsman doesn't become a new and different person for having chopped the wood. But one of the joys of parenting is that we can see growth—if only in ourselves. As our children grow, so do we. And it is this sense of personal growth that gives us the courage to continue.

◆

What I do, daily, for my children creates deep and immediate changes in me. Every day, I am stronger and wiser and more courageous because I am a parent.

Sometimes I would almost rather have people take away years of my life than take away a moment.
—*Pearl Bailey*

The moment is special. In a moment, you hear your baby cry, see him take his first steps, hear him call your name. The moment is real—and, as time goes, a lot more tangible than eternity.

It is difficult, in the hectic pace of our days, to grasp a concept so vast as sixty or seventy or eighty years. A lifetime of moments seems even harder to imagine, and harder still to recollect. But one moment—one special time when everything felt right and real and complete—this we can remember.

As parents, we need to understand the importance of a moment more than we need to keep track of the days of our lives.

◆

The concept of eternity may be difficult to grasp—but I can always find joy in a moment.

The secret of dealing successfully with a child is not to be its parent.

—*Mell Lazarus*

The irony of being a parent is that almost from the very beginning your kids seem to have more respect for the opinions of everyone else—friends, neighbors, screen idols. It's almost as if you were wearing the Scarlet Letter—something that branded you as "inconsequential" or "stupid." Nothing you say seems to be heard; nothing you do seems to be valued.

The truth is, kids need their parents, but in a different way than they need other adults. They need their parents to give them unconditional love and to offer them unwavering support and security. They do not need them to recommend a good TV show. For that, there's *TV Guide* and their three best friends.

The kind of things kids need from their parents are often hard to ask for. That's why parents need to see what isn't always visible and hear what isn't always said.

◆

My children may need me when I'm least aware of it. I will pay special attention to these needs, which often go unmet.

One of the most tragic things I know about human nature is that all of us tend to put off living. We are all dreaming of some magical rose garden over the horizon—instead of enjoying the roses that are blooming outside our windows today.

—*Dale Carnegie*

Perhaps, as we try to carve out time and space for our children, we feel that we are sacrificing other goals and dreams. We might have been more successful lawyers or writers or businessmen if we had worked longer hours. We have sacrificed so much to be parents, and we wonder, as we dream of that "magical rose garden over the horizon" if we will ever have a second chance.

We must remember that our children are the here and now, the "roses that are blooming outside our windows today." What they are to us now they can never be again. If we do not take the time to find the joy in these moments of their youth, all we will have are photographs of memories filed away in scrapbooks.

◆

Dreams cannot compare with the reality my children offer to me. If I enjoy what is in my life today, I may create new dreams for the future.

Only a mediocre person is always at his best.
—*W. Somerset Maugham*

As parents, we are not all that different from athletes-in-training. Some days our energy level is high and we feel there is nothing—no sprint, backhand, backflip or backstroke—we cannot do. Other days, we are run-down, our emotions depleted, our bodies exhausted. We need to rest and take the time to restore our spirit.

Pushing and striving every day to maximize our performance does not guarantee greatness—on the contrary, it ensures mediocrity. We must learn that to be at our "personal best," we may have to experience some days at our personal worst.

◆

I cannot be in top form every day; I can parent more effectively if I allow myself to recycle my energy.

If it ain't broke, don't fix it.

—*Old adage*

It's eight o'clock in the evening. The kids are home, supper's done, the dishes are put away, and we're gathered around our favorite TV show. It seems a blissful picture. But we can't quite relax. We think "something is wrong." There has to be something here that I need to "fix."

As parents who do too much, we like to think that there is nothing we can't make just a little bit better, no situation we can't improve upon. Nothing is beyond our range; we're always on call, and many times we "act" before we get "the call."

But we need to learn to let well enough alone. When we try to mend what doesn't need fixing, we may end up creating more problems than we solve.

◆

Isn't it great that sometimes my children are getting along just fine?

> I really believe there are things nobody would see if I didn't photograph them.
>
> —*Diane Arbus*

Arbus was right; there are so many things we don't see because we are too busy to notice them.

If I open my eyes and look around, really look around, I see so much. All of it is there for the taking. I do not have to learn how to see the grass or the sky or faces in the clouds. I do not need a degree in engineering to watch a plane fly overhead and understand its beauty.

There are so many things life has to offer, so much joy that is ours for the taking.

◆

Today I will take time to look at life and, perhaps, see it as if for the first time. Rushing through life denies me so much.

The thing that must survive you is not just the record of your practice, but the principles of your practice.

—*Bernice Johnson Reagon*

In future years, when people speak of your achievements, do you want them to hold up a stack of calendars, several inches thick, showing a record of all you did and where you went to do it? "Here's the kind of parent I was—look at all I got done!"

Or would you rather they spoke of your kindness and creativity, the principles that guided you through parenting and helped you raise happy, healthy children?

Viewed in this way, we realize how important it is for us to have a guiding principle, a parenting philosophy that takes us through our days. Otherwise, we are nothing more than robots, completing the necessary daily tasks.

◆

I am not a robot. I am a thinking, feeling, caring person with beliefs and principles.

Our family was not so much socially uninteresting as socially uninterested. If life is in some sense a status race, my parents never noticed the flag drop.

—*Joseph Epstein*

When your first child is born, the race begins. You have a choice: Start running as fast as you can—or drop out. It's up to you.

If you choose not to run, the "racers" will try to make you feel guilty. (You're not sending your son to sleep-away camp?) (You're not looking into private school?) (Your daughter doesn't take piano lessons?) Threatened by your lack of concern over these things, your disinterest in the socially acceptable, parentally "responsible" choices, they will attempt to goad you into joining them.

Be aware that once you do, it's difficult to stop. Everyone around you is running as fast as possible, jockeying for better position, building up more and more stamina in preparation for the home stretch. It's a race to the finish, and the winner may lose all.

◆

When parenthood becomes a race for status and prestige, the children always lose.

People who fight fire with fire usually end up with ashes.

—Abigail Van Buren

War, whether it is waged on the battlefield, or in our own homes, is hell. The antidote for war is peace. If I promote peace in my home, if I speak more softly, ask more kindly, share more responsibly, teach less aggressively, I am promoting the kind of atmosphere in which growth is possible.

When anger is out of control in our homes, we create "out of control" children who cannot solve problems except by raising their voices or using their fists.

It is difficult not to "fight fire with fire," to meet our children's raised voices with raised voices of our own, but we must try. Otherwise, the cycle will be repeated again, generation to generation.

◆

I don't want to wage war in my home. Today I will make an effort to restore peace.

Our greatest danger in life is in permitting the urgent thing to crowd out the important.

—*Charles E. Hummel*

As parents who do too much, we are often prioritizing. We will put aside the medical checkup, the long-distance call to a friend—because there are "important" things to get done—things that need our immediate attention.

But let us not confuse urgency with importance. Just because something sits up and begs at our feet, does not mean we have to throw it a bone.

The things we get done first are usually the ones that are least important but most persistent—the phone calls, the shopping, the cleaning—the list of "must do's." The really important things—time spent with our children, for example—may get put on hold.

◆

I may not be the best judge of what is truly important in my life. Today I'll juggle the schedule a bit and see if I can't change the order of things.

While everything else in our lives has gotten simpler, speedier, more microwavable and user-friendly, child-raising seems to have expanded to fill the time no longer available for it.

—*Barbara Ehrenreich*

Of course, raising children is a little tougher than making popcorn. Still, it would be nice if in this technological age we had some pop-up, zip-lock, foolproof guide to getting our kids to adulthood.

In this "age of opportunity," when everything seems possible, we are forced into a pace that is out of sync with human capacity. If child raising has "expanded to fill the time" we no longer have, it may be because we are trying to raise our children so that they can survive in this challenging and complicated new world.

But despite the fact that civilization has hit an all-time record for breakneck pace, despite the innovation of cars and faxes and airplanes and computers, we're seemingly no better off than we were.

◆

I am a human being, not a computer. Today I will function at the top of my capacity and not one microsecond more.

It seems to me that we are doing things we do not want to do for kids who do not really want to have them done.

—*Robert Paul Smith*

There's a classic "Twilight Zone" episode about a gambler who dies and ends up in a place where all he does, all day long, is gamble and win. Having everything he's always dreamed of becomes his worst nightmare, his private Hell.

If we are "doing things" for our kids out of a sense of obligation or guilt, we need to examine these motives. "Things" do not replace love and laughter. Buying your son Super-Nintendo doesn't replace throwing the ball with him in the backyard. Giving your daughter sailing lessons doesn't take the place of reading her stories at bedtime.

When we can't spend enough time with our children, we must not replace ourselves with "things." We give them the amount of time we have available and, from the smiles on their faces, we know that it is enough.

◆

The greatest gift I give my children is the time I spend with them.

There's no present. There's only the immediate future and the recent past.

—*George Carlin*

There is no "present" for us parents who do too much. There is only past and future. If we take time to stop, in the midst of our whirlwind schedule, we can tell you what we just "did," and what we now "have to do." We are going from "here" to get to "there." We are not experiencing life; we are only living it.

To live in the present requires commitment. We have to be awake and alive, able to see what is around us. We cannot just drive past the lake on the way to work; we have to appreciate the beauty of the lake as we see the sunrise reflected in its depths. We cannot just "hear" our children's voices; we have to listen to what they are saying.

◆

To be fixated on the past or focused on the future prevents me from experiencing the joy of the present.

Forget goals. Value the process.

—*Jim Bouton*

Bouton was talking about his game—baseball—but we can just as easily and appropriately apply this to the rule of our game—parenthood. Goals are distant and often unattainable. They link us to a chain of events, bind us to a prescribed plan.

We feel freer to enjoy the process of parenthood if we do not set unreachable goals for ourselves. Our children benefit from the ease in our attitudes, the lilt to our steps. They feel less like "projects" and more like companions.

In parenthood, as in baseball, we need to put aside the "game plan" and think, instead, about the value of just playing the game.

◆

I have much to gain from my everyday role as a parent if I can relinquish my attachment to distant goals.

[Family] bonds are formed less by moments of cele-
bration and of crisis than by the quiet, undramatic ac-
cretion of minutiae—the remark on the way out the
door, the chore undone, the unexpected smile.
—*George Howe Colt*

As parents who do too much, we pour a great deal of
energy into "events"—birthdays, bar mitzvahs, wed-
dings. And we are always available to charge into a crisis situation at a moment's notice. Perhaps we feel that
these are the important things—the things we'll one
day look back on and remember.

The truth is, it is daily life, the little things we often
overlook or take for granted, that we will one day miss.

Have you ever leafed through your childhood photo
album? You scanned the photographs of birthdays
(that's you, blowing out the candles) and vacations
(that's you, at the Grand Canyon), but you found yourself fixated on the tiniest details: a stuffed toy in the
corner, the pattern of the living-room wallpaper, an or-
nament on the Christmas tree, the curl of your father's
mustache.

◆

*I will try to pay attention to the "details" of my life. These
are the things I will someday wish I could remember.*

My child looked at me and I looked back at him in the delivery room, and I realized that out of a sea of infinite possibilities it had come down to this: a specific person, born on the hottest day of the year, conceived on a Christmas Eve, made by his father and me miraculously from scratch.

—*Anna Quindlen*

It is amazing. This child, handed to us in the delivery room, is ours and is like no other child, ever. It is our responsibility to raise it and nurture it. There are no other parents like us, ever.

These are awesome concepts, and, if we think about them, they boggle the mind. Sometimes the sheer majesty of it all is overwhelming—even numbing. It makes us feel incredibly proud and incredibly afraid—all at the same time. We have responsibility for this life!

Still, even if it is amazing, it happens every day, every hour, every minute—in some hospital, in some city, in some country of the world. We are parents and we are all bound together in a miraculous, confounding journey.

◆

I will try not to let my awe of this child prevent me from grounding myself in the reality of everyday life.

Bringing up a family should be an adventure, not an anxious discipline in which everybody is constantly graded for performance.

—*Milton R. Sapirstein*

It would help if we understood that we're all in it together—our children and us. We're a unit, a family, rowing the same boat in an effort to reach the shore. When we row in unison, in rhythm, we are confident we will get there; when we row out of turn, against each other, we are in danger of capsizing.

Still, we cannot be too hard on ourselves. This is an adventure, not a contest. Adrift on the high seas, we are buffeted about by strong currents and tides that shift without warning. We cannot expect ourselves to be always upright, always equal to the task. We're inexperienced adventurers, a family adrift, but still afloat.

◆

If I see this as an adventure, I will think of the difficult parts as progress.

The average family exists only on paper and its average budget is a fiction, invented by statisticians for the convenience of statisticians.

—*Sylvia Porter*

Parents who do too much may be striving to live up to some ideal picture of "the family" created by the "experts."

The truth is, there is no such thing as the "ideal" children or the "ideal" parents. There is no "how it ought to be"; there is only "how it is." We have to do this one step at a time, using whatever method seems appropriate to the moment, hoping that the new approach we've just invented works. Sure, we may get ideas from colleagues and friends and even "experts." But, in the end, its every parent for himself.

When the experts and the poll takers tell us one thing, we should probably tune it out. Statisticians and theorists don't raise children; parents raise children.

◆

I need to give myself credit for knowing what is best for my family.

The most exhausting thing in life is being insincere.
—*Anne Morrow Lindbergh*

When we are false, when we wear a mask for our children, we feel exhausted. There is always an image to live up to, a fiction to create. We cannot enjoy our days, because we might step out of character, let down our guard for a moment.

Parents who do too much need to be able to find comfort and security in their home life. Otherwise, they run from one pressure cooker to another, from the dreaded office to the dreaded family room.

Our homes need to sanctify and preserve. Our children need to accept us for who we are, to know that we are human and that all of our failures are human failures.

◆

I will give myself the freedom to let my children see me as I really am.

One ought every day at least, to hear a little song, read a good poem, see a fine picture, and, if it were possible, to speak a few reasonable words.
—*Johann Wolfgang von Goethe*

What Goethe wrote sounds so simple. It doesn't seem too much to ask—to find time for these simple things. Yet, it is the simple things that are shoved aside in these fast-paced times. We seem to find a great deal of time for complexity—for financial schemes and kitchen wizardry—but no time at all for simplicity.

Parents, especially, are burdened by complexity. When we have children, we suddenly have added responsibilities for the future. A few moments listening to music or reading or writing seems too much to ask when there are "real issues" to be addressed, pressing needs to be met.

And yet, if we deny ourselves the simple pleasures, if we turn our backs on life's quiet gifts, aren't we cheating ourselves out of self-fulfillment?

◆

Accepting the simple things life has to offer me is like handing myself special gifts that are there for the taking.

Be not angry that you cannot make others as you wish to be, since you cannot make yourself as you wish to be.

—*Thomas à Kempis*

You may as well resign yourself to the fact that your children will not grow up as you wish them to be. If you think about your own life, you know how much was left to chance—and timing. Of course, you prepared yourself for life—but you couldn't plan everything. Life is not a planned event; life happens.

If this lack of control makes you feel helpless, it shouldn't. Part of the joy, the richness, of life is spontaneity. The unexpected is often the most treasured, the unplanned event often the most joyous. Why deny our children the right to enjoy life as it happens? Why deny ourselves the right to be open to these possibilities?

It is easier for us to let go of our children, if we understand that our control over their lives is a myth.

◆

If I cannot create my children's lives the way I wish them to be, I will try to stand back and admire them for what they are.

Guilt: the gift that keeps on giving.

—*Erma Bombeck*

When we do too much for our children, it is probably out of guilt. This is the legacy we received from our parents, and the one that, if we are not careful, we may pass on to our own children.

Guilt springs from feelings of insecurity and self-doubt. We do not feel guilty when we trust in our own conduct, our own code of behavior. It is when we listen to others telling us what to do and what not to do that we become confused and suffer from feelings of inadequacy.

When we feel guilty, it is because we don't feel that we are good enough; we don't trust ourselves. We must remember that confidence is gained through our own action and reaction, not by repeating the mistakes of the past.

◆

If I do as my own parents did, I may be repeating unhealthy patterns; I will try to have more confidence in my own ability to act.

Listening to your children is like shopping in the bargain basement; you get a lot of things you didn't know you needed—and at a very good price.

—*Anonymous*

We turn to just about everyone for guidance: talk-show guests, self-help experts, our best friend's best friend, the man behind us in the checkout line at the grocery store. Everyone has something to teach us about parenting. But, for some reason, the last person we'll turn to is the first person we ought to: our child.

She has a lot to teach us, if we'll listen. After all, it's her life we're concerned about, her future we're planning. We need to think of her as an ally, at least, a consultant, at best. She can tell us, among other things, whether we're on the right track.

Our children may not have all the answers, but they're likely to help us reformulate the questions.

◆

I don't know what my children are thinking unless I ask. Today I'll talk to them before I talk to the "experts."

. . . . when I was a tiny child I turned from the window out of which I was watching a snowstorm and hopefully asked, "Momma, do we believe in Winter?"
—*Philip Roth*

It is wonderful that we share our beliefs with our children. But it is also important for us to encourage them to think for themselves. The freedom of the human mind and spirit is a good and necessary thing.

It is important for our children to have a sense of family, of "where I come from." But parents who do too much to ensure their child's strict adherence to family beliefs, may be denying, at an early age, a child's right to question, to think for himself.

Whether we are Jews or Catholics or Muslims or Zen Buddhists, our children must be encouraged to explore and understand the doctrines we pass along, not merely accept, without questioning, what we hand down to them.

◆

If I try too hard to indoctrinate my children, I may be taking away their right to independent thought.

It has become more important to be a smart kid than a good kid or even a healthy kid.

—*Sam Levenson*

Levenson said this when we were back in grade school—so many of us being herded like good little cattle, into "bright" or "slow" classrooms according to that frighteningly powerful measuring device, the I.Q. score.

Now we may be passing on this pressure for intellectual achievement to our children. We want our Johnny and our Jane to read before they enter kindergarten, to add and subtract and multiply before they can count!

We may need to reevaluate our measure of success. What is good for Johnny and Jane may have little to do with the size of their Iowa or SAT scores, and much more to do with their own personal sense of well-being, their moral and spiritual values and concern for their fellow man.

◆

The goals and standards I have set for my children may have more to do with what was expected of me than what I now perceive may be right for them.

Your children are not your children.

They are the sons and daughters of life's longing for itself.

They come through you but not from you.

And though they are with you yet they belong not to you.

—*Kahlil Gibran*

Possessiveness is a trait known well to overcommitted, obsessive parents. We all too often assume, because of our need to control, that we are the masters of our children now and in the future.

But our children are in many ways totally independent of us. We need to be more aware of who they are and of what they are capable.

When we believe our children are mere extensions of ourselves, we annihilate their individuality. Our children are unique unto themselves, and need not be judged by who *we* are.

◆

I want to remember to treat my children with kindness, simplicity, and freedom throughout this day.

I'm dancing as fast as I can.

—*Barbara Gordon*

Parents who do too much take great pride in how fast we do it. We need to learn that there is no particular honor in "getting there first"—except during an Olympic marathon.

In this society, we are so bent on accomplishing all our tasks as quickly as possible, that we rarely, if ever, think about the enjoyment of our work, how it may enrich us, or what we may learn from it. Rather, we're immersed in getting it "done." And what has that "done" to us?

◆

The demands we have placed upon one another to perform recklessly and with ferocity have killed our enjoyment and fulfillment in our work. This takes a toll on me personally, but also on my children and my spouse.

Have the courage to be ignorant of a great number of things, in order to avoid the calamity of being ignorant of everything.

—*Sydney Smith*

Those of us who do too much also think we know it all. Because we're so overcommitted it must follow that we're burdened by our knowledge and only activity can satisfy us. This is, of course, a myth.

Often we're camouflaging our ignorance by activity and promise. We need to have the courage to be ignorant and not allow ourselves to be imprisoned by information. If we need the props that being all-knowing gives us, then we have overdressed the set, and the play that follows will be calamitous and incoherent.

◆

Teaching my children, by example, that ignorance is no vice, and may only be temporary, is a real gift.

When we can begin to take our failures non-seriously, it means we are ceasing to be afraid of them. It is of immense importance to learn to laugh at ourselves.
—*Katherine Mansfield*

Fear of failure, indecision, and the thought that all of our parenting "methods" are final and inflexible, take a major toll on us. We see our task as a grave duty, and we become hardened and fearful.

If we can get enough of a perspective on our parenting and not be such harsh judges of our human frailties, we can begin to see that our fears are self-fulfilling prophecies, and that a good deal of what we fear is unimportant in the larger scheme of bringing up our children.

◆

To treat everything with the same amount of gravity is self-defeating. I want to feel free enough to step back and be unafraid of every decision I make.

The perfectionist is a man whom it is impossible to please because he is never pleased with himself.
—*Johann Wolfgang von Goethe*

Parents who do too much are never pleased with their own performances. That is why we set such unattainable standards for our children. When we do this, we undermine what could be a warmer, sunnier climate in which our children can grow.

The shadow cast by a perfectionist parent is a long one. It inhibits the ecology of the family by creating an environment that may only produce stunted growth—withered children, who in turn can never hope to live up to anyone's—not even their own—expectations.

◆

One of the terrible hazards of living in such a demanding, fast-paced, goal-oriented time, is that we maintain impossible measures of success which, ironically, breeds little but failure. I do not want my perfectionism to hamper my children's growth.

Q: What do you call someone who graduated in last place in his class at medical school?

A: A doctor.

—*Anonymous*

There are so many qualities that make us "good" parents. I don't think most of these attributes can be measured. Can you be graded on kindness, patience, sensitivity, love or strength of character? Not really, because the combination of those attributes, the collage of qualities we offer our children, creates a patchwork of who we are.

The rigors of self-judgment and societal judgment are harsh and artificial. No one has all the answers, all the talents, and nobody is a perfect parent.

◆

I am fallible and not always quantifiable. I need to remind myself of my strengths, especially during times of weakness.

If a man aspires to the highest place, it is no dishonor to him to halt at the second, or even at the third.
—*Cicero*

Over the course of years of watching the Olympics, we have noticed a not-so-subtle shift in the attitude of many of the athletes. Now, more than ever, it seems that those who don't win the gold feel that they have failed entirely.

When young women and men are interviewed (some seem more like children than adults) they speak of winning a silver or a bronze medal nearly with disgust. And, everyday, during the Olympic trials, there, right on the front page of many of our nation's newspapers, is a box that shows how many gold medals the United States has garnered—only the gold. This promotes a debilitating attitude that says: "If I'm not first, I've failed completely."

◆

I will try not to put too much emphasis on winning. I do not want my children to be dispirited when they come in second, fifth, or last in anything they try.

Mistakes are a fact of life. It is the response to error that counts.

—*Nikki Giovanni*

As children, we were probably not forgiven too many "mistakes." We need to teach our children that life is about a variety of experiences, including "error."

Gently and artfully explaining to a child that he or she has slipped up is important, because early on we may be setting ourselves up for an adversarial relationship with our children by judging too harshly and punishing too swiftly. We need to ask ourselves "Why?" before we ask our children "How?"

◆

In attempting to instill the acceptance of error in our children, we first must demonstrate our flexibility and facility in dealing with our own.

'Tis always morning somewhere in the world.
—Richard Henry Horne

And the sun will come up and shine through our windows again. We need to remind ourselves of this when we feel at wit's end, when we believe that we've done "all we can do," and are emotionally spent.

Things change. A child who has low self-esteem may one day end up the president of his class. When things seem to be insurmountable, when we feel at our most helpless, we must remember that tomorrow will give us another chance to help bring about change—to look at the situation with a new eye.

◆

Hope is an important part of parenting. Today is the first day of the rest of my child's life.

The more people have studied different methods of bringing up children, the more they have come to the conclusion that what good mothers and fathers instinctively feel like doing for their babies is the best after all.

—*Benjamin Spock*

When we had our first child, we nearly cleaned off the parenting and childcare shelves in our local bookstore before the blessed event was six months away.

Penelope Leach, Fitzhugh Dodson, Lee Salk, and Berry Brazelton—we had all of their works, and books by many others as well. We had so overprepared ourselves to parent that much of the information we got from these books became a not-so-harmonious mix of professionals canceling out one another's philosophies. We had a cacophony of expert voices in our heads.

After our second child was born we relied far more on our experience, trusting in our love and intuition.

◆

If I give myself enough time to ponder a problem, or make a decision, most of the time I'll do what is right for my child.

The art of being wise is the art of knowing what to overlook.

—*William James*

Parents who do too much often don't know how to modulate their attention to their children. Every breath their child takes is an occasion to render a judgment or create a worry.

For all of our best intentions in attempting to instill table manners, polite conversation, appropriate behaviors of all kinds, we sometimes burden our children with too much stage direction.

We need to pull back, allow them to breathe on their own, let the small things go, and not direct every moment of their day. Otherwise, we become hostage to our children and to our over-parenting.

◆

I'm going to be conscious of what to overlook. I want to give my family a chance to grow without "breathing lessons."

The beginning of wisdom is to call things by their right names.

—*Chinese proverb*

When we're at our perfectionist worst we tend to be blindsided by it. When our children are crying out for help by acting out at school or by shoplifting and lying, we need to stop and call the problem what it is.

Too often, we hide our fear of what our children are trying to tell us about themselves or about their relationship with us, and so we refer to these events as "just teenage rebellion" or "just a phase," or "just childhood laziness."

Parents who do too much often do not do enough introspection. Are we afraid of what we might find if we look too deep?

◆

In order for me to be successful and happy in my parenting, I need to discover what my problems might be. I don't want to promote lives that are lived in euphemism.

The battle to keep up appearances unnecessarily, the mask—whatever name you give creeping perfectionism—robs us of our energies.

—*Robin Worthington*

We've been so busy being perfect that the house has come down on our heads. The last coat of paint we used to cover the cracks in the walls didn't stop the roof from caving in. And so our perfection, our workaholism, our need to seem complete and without fault has doubled back on us, pinning us under a mound of rubble, sealing our fate.

The energy we put out in disguising the encroaching terror diminished our ability to do exactly what we wanted to do—be good parents—not perfect ones.

◆

Every family has its troubles, but denying them, and camouflaging them with smiles and pats on the back will encourage eventual damage.

Not what we have, but what we enjoy, constitutes an abundance.

—*Anonymous*

Most of us spent the eighties attaining "things." And we could rationalize our binge on gadgets, tools, and the best educational toys because, after all, "it's for the kids."

Some of us now have a mountain of accumulated things that seemed totally necessary a few years ago. Our basements appear to be a distribution center for Toys-R-Us. It's not just that our children outgrew much of what we bought. That is inevitable. It's that a great deal of these things were never used or never enjoyed.

Now we know that the things our children really enjoyed were the times we spent together—talking, sharing, laughing, and getting to know each other.

◆

I am a parent with great abundance. I have a wealth of memories and a rich future to look forward to.

How glorious it is—and how painful also—to be an exception.

—*Alfred de Musset*

When we do our best to allow our children to become who they need to be, not what we need them to be, there is a risk. The risk is that they may choose a lifestyle or a career that is not a "mainstream" or wholly "acceptable" or "acknowledged" path. In so doing they may suffer ridicule, isolation, and loneliness.

What we need to do is simply remind them that the road not taken is without question a rewarding route, even if it is one with little traffic.

◆

I will not attempt to thwart my child's interest for the sake of society. Each child is unique and must live his own life.

Some people seem as if they could never have been children, and others seem as if they could never be anything else.

—*George Dennison Prentice*

To lose sight of what it was like to be a child—the wonderment, the laughter with abandon, the carefree summers, is to forget the essence of openness, of clear unadulterated thought, and unencumbered kindness. We've all seen these people—they're intolerant, unyielding, joyless, and often, workaholics.

The reverse can be as spiritless. When we grow up, but not internally, and do not grasp the lessons that life must teach us in order to pass them along to our children, we become our child's peer—a dangerous and inappropriate thing to be. Remembering the joy of childhood is not the same as repeating it.

◆

The key is balance. I can keep the joy of childhood alive within me even though I am an adult.

When you have gained a victory, do not push it too far.

—*Eustace Budgell*

When we have been successful in negotiating with our child, and we win out, and our child acquiesces to our way of thinking, it is important for us not to belittle our children and use that victory to deflate their egos.

Parenting is about "letting go" and knowing when to yield to a child's need to be self-reliant and independent. If we are always feeling the need to claim victory over every confrontation, we will have children who finally will resent us, but will never be able to leave us.

◆

I will try turning away after I've "won the battle." Hammering away at my child diminishes both of us.

There is nothing more poetic in the freshness of its passions than a sixteen-year-old heart. The morning of life is like the dawn of a day, full of purity, vision, and harmony.

—*Chateaubriand*

And as parents, how our hearts ache when we see both the promise of that child's heart, and the pain we know it must bear.

Parents who do too much often, without realizing it, try to live the lives of their children—for them—not just because they want to live those early years again vicariously, but because they want to spare their children from the pain of growing up.

Purity of heart and openness of mind is truly a wonderful thing to see and, if we do not discourage it or frighten it, an energizing force to be near.

◆

I do not want to control my child's early years as a young adult. I do want to warn her of some of the dangers out there, but not to the extent that she dreads the next part of her life.

A graceful taunt is worth a thousand insults.
—*Louis Nizer*

As our children begin to understand and develop a sense of humor, and exhibit an ability to use it appropriately, it can be a powerful means of communicating with them.

Insulting our children, with mean-spirited sarcasm, flaunting our verbal abilities, makes them feel terrible—it demeans them and makes them feel worthless. They learn nothing from this kind of cruelty and criticism.

But joking with them, verbal sparring on their level, shows them that in some ways you see them as equals. This helps build self-confidence and mutual respect.

◆

We live in a time when biting wit and abrasive sarcasm can be heard on every TV and on every car radio. Gentle "ribbing" is hard to establish, but I want to bring that to my family. It may enrich all of us.

We build statues out of snow, and weep to see them melt.

—*Walter Scott*

When we see our children, do we perceive them as who they are, or have we made them mythical characters—set up monuments to them in our minds—all out of proportion to reality?

Sometimes parents who do too much also fantasize too much, and cannot see their children as they really are. We want certain things so desperately for them—great talent, high intelligence, creativity, that we sometimes imagine more than truly exists.

◆

I need to be realistic about my children's strengths and weaknesses. Otherwise, it will be difficult to hide my disappointment when they cannot live up to my expectations.

She felt in italics and thought in capitals.

—*Henry James*

Overcommitted parents are often high-pitched, emotional, and melodramatic. Because we put so much energy into life, everything is heightened for us—experiences are exaggerated—and soon, all of life, from the meaningful to the trivial, takes on the same deafening level of importance.

We need to learn modulation. Not everything is worthy of a proclamation, and the grandiosity that is revealed by this self-important demeanor surely exposes our need to "be the best," and to call attention to every detail of our lives.

◆

When all the instruments in the orchestra are at full volume, there is no melody; there is only noise.

Just think of the tragedy of teaching children not to doubt.

—*Clarence Darrow*

One of the problems with being an overcommitted parent is that the art of conversation is almost always lost.

After all, who has the time to discuss the day's events, the current political scene, or anything the children want to talk about? Because we are all on an information overload, we have little time to weigh or decipher all of the "stuff" that's thrown at us. We have little time to question.

But questioning begets thought. And thought begets conversation, the sharing of one's insights and opinions. What a terrible and lonely world it would be if we were no longer to teach our children, by example, to question.

◆

I do not want to instill in my children the belief that every source of information is reliable, including things said by their teachers and their parents. Doubt is healthy.

Don't say yes till I've finished talking.
—*Anonymous*

When we're in a rush—and who isn't?—we tend to speak to our children in shorthand, spewing off dictates, rules, jobs, and schedules. When we do this, we teach our children to respond to us in shorthand.

In the exaggerated and overburdened society we live in, it seems crucial to give immediate, if neither accurate nor correct, answers.

The irony is, in the rush to communicate, we rarely get across what we want to say. And we certainly don't engender the responses we need.

◆

If I do not want to pass along to my child the drill-sergeant-method of learning and responding, I need to act like someone who has the time for real communication.

He did not care in which direction the car was traveling, so long as he remained in the driver's seat.
—*Lord Beaverbrook*

Some of us have such a need to control others (our children, our spouses, our co-workers) that we become engrossed in the mechanics of accomplishment and forget what we had set out to accomplish.

If we fear losing control, it is because we are sure that once we do we will have to face ourselves, our faults, and our failures. And so we hold on, in desperation, keeping it all together under the protective banner of parenthood.

No one is more cocksure of himself than a parent who does too much.

◆

If I'm to lead the way along with my spouse, I will need to consult each of my family members in order to find out which way we shall proceed.

After the pain of parting comes the happiness of healing; rediscovering life, friends, self. Joy.
> —*Harold Bloomfield, Melba Cosgrove,*
> *and Peter McWilliams*

When our children are ready to leave our homes, they needn't leave our hearts. We know it is the normal course of events, the appropriate evolution, but we try to hold on. This can be painful, for both parent and child.

If we begin to "rediscover" ourselves, rekindling old friendships, making new ones, and becoming comfortable with the idea that our children are now adults, we will be able to get on with the next phase of our lives.

◆

I hope I can be clear-headed and healthy enough to let go of my children when they become adults. I may feel "empty," but it will only be a temporary emptiness.

Outside noisy, inside empty.

—Chinese proverb

When we live our lives totally on the exterior and never stop long enough for introspection, reflection, or self-assessment, it usually is a sign that we have over-committed ourselves to others. Too often that leads to emotional malnutrition. The lights are on, but nobody's home.

Giving of ourselves to our children need not mean giving up on ourselves. Just because we have children does not mean we cease to be people in our own right.

Those of us who are given to doing too much often employ the art of dodging life by appearing to be totally immersed in it.

◆

Beware the parent (and I may look in the mirror if I need to) who makes all the noise, but who is an absentee mother or father.

The thing I liked least about my mother was that she was always giving the most.

—Anonymous

A martyr or a saint is hard to live with or live up to. When you give and give and give to your children, you are exacting a terrible price from them, constantly reminding them of your sacrifice.

When you "suffer the most" you are giving your children a constant reminder of what you have given up for them—and they may, consciously or otherwise, begin to wonder if they were worth it.

◆

I will try to be mindful not to saddle my children with the burden of appreciation and gratitude.

The whole life of the individual is nothing but the process of giving birth to himself; indeed, we should be fully born when we die—although it is the tragic fate of most individuals to die before they are born.

—*Erich Fromm*

We have been taught that there are certain age-appropriate times for the beginning and the end of our development. We have been tyrannized by an outmoded, archaic notion that we have only one career per life, that we must have our children before thirty-five, retire at sixty-five, and not question the cycles of life too rigorously.

Parents who do too much often submit to this imaginary arc of one's life. We think that the pattern of our lives is, for the most part, fully prescribed—and that its ebb and flow is subject not to our own desires and wishes, but to a certain life standard we must adhere to.

◆

Let me not conform to chronologies that have little to do with my own wants and needs. I need to open to the rebirth of the self at any age.

> If you scatter thorns, don't go barefoot.
> —*Italian proverb*

We know we reap what we sow. This is especially true in relation to our children—when, as parents, what we say and do may come back to haunt us.

Sometimes it is difficult for us to see the many ways in which we influence our children. Unknowingly, we may poison their attitudes or views about a friend or relative—as the result, of perhaps, a long-standing grudge. Even our political views, our attitudes about money and sex and friendship and the environment, may resurface, in one form or another, in our children.

◆

I must be careful about how I demonstrate my views. What I say and do—and how I say it and do it—will have a profound effect on my children.

Trust your heart....Never deny it a hearing. It is the kind of house oracle that often foretells the most important.

—*Baltasar Gracián*

When parents who do too much overthink a problem, second-guess themselves to death, and begin doubting their instincts, it is time to begin the journey back to the heart.

Most of us instinctively know when we've made the right decision. But when the head rules, when we overanalyze all of our parenting decisions, that is when self-doubt prevails.

Our children are bound to gain more from our honest answers, from the decisions that come freely from the heart.

◆

When my heart rules, I am more often than not comfortable with my choices.

October 1

Children's talent to endure stems from their ignorance of alternatives.

—*Maya Angelou*

Parents who do too much are often constrained by freedom, bound to the shackles of free will. Possibilities
surround us, opportunity calls. Now that we're grown-
ups, we can do so much and all at the same time; yet
we end up paralyzed by these choices, trapped by the
overcommitment our freedom engenders.

Our children endure because they have nothing else to
do but endure. There is an appealing simplicity to
their lives, an honesty to their straightforward decision-making. Because they cannot go left or right or
backward, they walk straight up the middle, with incredible ease.

◆

*I will try not to let the alternatives that are available to
me become the means of my self-destruction.*

The young do not know enough to be prudent, and therefore they attempt the impossible—and achieve it, generation after generation.

—*Pearl S. Buck*

It is not what they know—but rather what they seek—that carries our children forward. Their dreams are fresh and alive, while ours are on the top shelf of the closet, packed away with our old clothes.

We take our job seriously. As parents we try to "be prudent," to think about safety and caution and planning and conscience. As parents, we step into new clothing, which is at first uncomfortable but finally fits us as if tailor-made. We no longer "attempt the impossible" because we must deal with what is practical and attainable and right around the next corner.

Still, every now and then, we need to pull down our dreams from the closet shelf, dust them off, and relive them, if only for an hour or two. We can still make them happen, if we believe we can.

◆

As a parent, I have so many responsibilities. Nevertheless, I must give myself time to imagine the possibilities.

One face to the world, another at home, makes for misery.

—*Amy Vanderbilt*

Many parents lead two lives. In one, we're expected to be dedicated, highly skilled professionals. In the other, our home life, we're expected to be warm, caring family members.

Many of us take off one hat and put on the other with such speed and acuity that we sometimes forget which "character" we're in. At times like these, we realize the difficulty of changing roles, the mental price we pay for our flawless performance.

We need to learn how to adapt to our various roles without completely changing our personas. We can be all of the wonderful things we are—wherever we are—without fear of exposure or ridicule.

◆

Whether I find myself with my colleagues or my patients or my clients or my children, the person I am is the person I must be.

When you take the bull by the horns—what happens is a tossup.

—*William Pett Ridge*

When we confront our children, forcing their hand, we often get more than we bargained for. "Where were you last night?" or "Did you really study for that math test?" is often met with sarcasm, verbal defensiveness, or outright lying. Unable to come forth with what we expect from them, our children are often backed into a corner.

Sometimes we need to take a more moderate approach. If we already know the answer, do we really need to ask the question?

When our kids disappoint us, we must remember that they have probably also disappointed themselves. The further penalty of our disapproval or accusation is not only unnecessary, it's demeaning.

◆

Asking pointed questions and pointing an accusatory finger won't get me very far with my children; I must realize that they may be learning more from their own mistakes than I can ever teach them.

Children can stand vast amounts of sternness. They rather expect to be wrong, and are quite used to being punished. It is injustice, inequity, and inconsistency that kill them.

—*Robert F. Capon*

If we are overworked and overcommitted in all kinds of ways, we may not have the time or patience to be fair and consistent with our children. Setting down rules we forget to follow, issuing edicts we have no time to enforce, we teach our children that their lives are futile and hopeless.

Flexibility is wonderful; casualness is desirable. But helter-skelter, on-again-off-again parenting—parenting without focus or principle—is harmful, both to ourselves and our children.

If we want our children to believe that what they do in their lives can make a difference, if we want them to see that actions produce results, we need to be consistent in our demands and fair in our judgments.

◆

It matters less what I do for my children than that I do it with fairness and consistency.

Happiness is an imaginary condition, formerly often attributed by the living to the dead, now usually attributed by adults to children, and by children to adults.

—*Thomas Szasz*

As parents who are overloaded with responsibilities and commitments, we long for the "happiness" of our youth. If only we could be kids again, kicking down the road with only a bottle cap and a skate key in our pocket, not a care in the world.

How quickly we forget! We forget how hard it is to be a child, the fears and concerns that go along with innocence. We forget what it's like to be small and unprotected and face every day with the challenge of the unknown. We forget what it's like to face bullies on the playground and teasing on the bus.

Every age carries with it its burdens—and also its rewards. In longing for the "happiness" of our past, we may be missing the possibilities in the present.

◆

I will try not to attach too much nostalgia to my youth; I know that this time in my life has its own unique rewards and benefits.

They are ill discoverers that think there is no land when they can see nothing but sea.

—*Francis Bacon*

Parents who are overcommitted can't see beyond the next stack of messages, the next load of laundry, the next hurdle of responsibilities. We are overburdened with things we must do—things that cannot wait. Like Columbus and his crew, we're surrounded by water on all sides, no land in sight.

If there is no end to our responsibilities, no fork in the road, just an endless cycle of work to be done, we may need to impose our own breaks, however artificial they may be. We need to alter the routine every now and then—go to a movie, have a massage, join a protest, ride in a hot-air balloon. Whatever is unusual or different or novel or daring or just plain fun—we need to do for ourselves.

◆

Taking breaks from my daily routine may enable me to start fresh, with renewed dedication and purpose.

A child of five would understand this. Send somebody to fetch a child of five.

—*Groucho Marx*

If you've ever listened to two five-year-olds communicate, you know they are honest and direct with each other. So why all the fuss? When we have something to say to our kids, why not just say it? Do we really think they need all the machinations, the explanations, the songs and dances, the apologies we give them?

Parents who overexplain and overanalyze tend to forget that when you talk to children, it's best to keep it straight and simple. Children's minds are uncluttered and unencumbered. They see things for what they are. They can genuinely tell when we're trying to soften the news or bend the truth. So, in the long run, when dealing with children, it's best not to beat around the bush.

◆

What a relief to know that what is best for my children—honesty and simplicity—is also best and most satisfying for me.

What's gone and what's past help should be past grief.

—*William Shakespeare*

The last thing we overcommitted parents need to dwell on is past mistakes. The "shoulda's" and the "if only's" belong to yesterday, not today. If we are bogged down by crises of conscience and pangs of guilt, we cannot function as complete, healthy individuals because a part of ourselves is missing, left in the past.

If we are aware of the process, we know we have tomorrow courtesy of yesterday. One day follows the other, and the next and the next, on our path toward fulfillment. There is no right or wrong in this process; there is only the sum total of life events, the complete set of pieces that create a magnificent puzzle.

◆

If I am to move forward with confidence, I cannot allow myself to grieve over past mistakes.

You start by saying no to requests. Then if you have to go to yes, okay. But if you start with yes, you can't go to no.

—*Mildred Perlman*

When we say no, it is out of strength, not weakness. We have a position; we take a stand. We know and respect our boundaries, our limitations. We recognize and honor our sense of self-worth.

If our children and our colleagues and our friends see us as doormats, they begin to lose respect for us. Oh, they may continue to make their demands. Why not? People will always take advantage of what is freely given. Still, their "taking" may begin to make them feel guilty—while it makes us feel resentful. The cycle is a hard one to break.

If we are to respect ourselves as parents—as human beings—we need to begin to say no when we mean no.

◆

Giving in constantly to the demands of others is wearing me down. I will try to say no more often and see how good it feels.

When you're young, the silliest notions seem the greatest achievements.

—Pearl Bailey

Parents who give too much praise to their children may be setting up higher expectations, greater burdens. And children who are praised too much may live each day thinking they need to live up to their last great effort—the one that was noticed.

When children feel a sense of pride, it is usually linked to the silliest, smallest things: learning to whistle, mastering the doorbell, finding a new route to the candy store. They feel a sense of pride in things we may overlook or take for granted.

If we do offer praise to our children, perhaps it should be for a job or task or accomplishment *they* feel particularly good about—not one that just happens to meet our own standards.

◆

I sometimes forget what it is like to be a child—and to take such pride and joy in the little things of life.

Better is it that thou shouldest not vow, than that thou shouldest vow and not pay.

—*Ecclesiastes*

Parenting requires of us that we make commitments to our children; still, we have to be selective. We cannot be in two places at the same time, and thinking we can race home from a business conference so that we don't miss the opening act of the school play may not always be realistic.

Still, we want to be there for our children—wherever and whenever we can. We must strike a bargain with ourselves: We will do it when possible and not feel guilty when it is not possible. It is better to live up to the pledges we do make than to promise and promise—and never deliver.

◆

I need to be more realistic about what I can and cannot do for my children. I will try not to make promises I can't possibly keep.

There is a time for engagement and a time for withdrawal. A time to walk around the job. A time to contemplate it—and a time to just laugh at it.

—*Robert Townsend*

The seasons of a man's life are not unlike the seasons of parenthood. The days are cyclical, bringing us times of frenzy and times of much needed calm. We must let ourselves be carried by the natural flow of things—riding even the gentlest wave to shore.

As parents we are not always comfortable with the calm days; some of us want daily excitement and constant challenge. Parenthood does not provide it. There are times when we need to step back from our children, see them from a distance. We can't always be right with them, in the center of their lives.

We can do more for children if, once in a while, we allow ourselves to do less. There is value in these quiet moments, these hours of contemplation and withdrawal.

◆

Standing back provides a different view. Today I will take some moments for quiet contemplation.

When we are tired, we are attacked by ideas we con-
quered long ago.

—Friedrich Wilhelm Nietzsche

When we are exhausted, some of us yell at our children
or say things we will later regret. When we do these
things we are not acting out of strength but out of
weakness. Outmoded ideas, old habits, some of which
came from our own childhoods, slip back in to our con-
sciousness.

We may call these moments "lapses," and feel guilty
for having them. The truth is, we are tired. Our energy
is spent, and we are functioning on automatic pilot.
We move through the days like robots, getting the job
done without emotion or sympathy or passion.

◆

*Giving my mind and my body a rest may not be easy—but
neither is parenting.*

When we all think alike, no one is thinking.
—*Walter Lippmann*

As parents, we are also explorers. With the birth of each child, we forge new territory. There is a great deal to discover, each day, if we are open to it.

But discovery may require the abandonment of belief. If we are not willing to discard old habits, old principles, then we cannot move forward. If we follow the rules that were handed down to us and do not attempt to create new ones, we bog down our future with past methods and principles. It's a little like bringing a bow and arrow on a mission to space; what use is it?

The things we have learned from our parents and friends are certainly useful. But we must learn to rise to the call of our conscience, to heed the voice that comes from within.

◆

I am on an important mission. I must not leave myself behind.

In frenzied offices, on bumper-to-bumper freeways and on busy downtown streets, there has been a pervasive feeling that something is amiss; that it is all getting out of hand.

—*Amy Saltzman*

With more and more of us feeling "uneasy" on the fast track, we are recognizing the need for change. As Saltzman says, we may need to change our priorities, to seek new paths toward self-fulfillment.

This does not mean we must abandon our goals; it simply means we may have to examine alternate routes, find new and creative ways of achieving them. We can, for example, set up offices in our homes; we can choose jobs that require less time for commuting; we can change the way we view success.

There are many different roads that lead to self-satisfaction. When we feel stuck, it is because we have forgotten to examine these alternate routes to success.

◆

Today I will think about how I can get out of the fast lane. I am no longer sure it is where I need to be.

We can scare ourselves or inspire ourselves . . . . We are the architects of our own attitudes and experiences. We design the world by the way we choose to see it.
—*Barry Neil Kaufman*

This new day is filled with promise. We can enter it with confidence—see the good that we can create out of it—or we can destroy it at first glance, letting negative thoughts about our children and ourselves propel us into a tailspin.

It is all in the way we choose to see it. For we "choose" our happiness—it is not given to us. There is great power in this, if we recognize it.

Will we let the day overcome us with worry and fear about the future? Or will we reach out to the joyous moments that are here and now, ripe for the taking?

◆

I can choose to see the glass as half empty or half full; it is how I choose to see things today that will make a difference.

The young have no depth perception in time. Ten years back or ten years forward is an eternity.

—*Robert C. Alberts*

One reason we try to cram so much into our days is that we recognize how quickly they fly by. Our children, by contrast, seem the epitome of slowness, as if unaware that the clock is ticking.

We watch them, unnerved by their casualness. "Hurry up," we scold them. "Can't you move any faster?" But why should they? They can take their time, because time is not their enemy. As if to taunt us, they meander through the moments, in no special hurry to arrive wherever it is we think they have to go.

It helps us to understand that children have a different concept of time: Their "slowness" is born not out of laziness but rather out of a sense of joy and abandon.

◆

I can see that my children are in less of a hurry; perhaps I should try my best to slow down so that they can keep up with me.

Make the best use of what is in your power, and take the rest as it happens.

—*Epictetus*

When we feel emotionally depleted, our bodies and minds exhausted by the day's activities, we feel powerless to control our lives. What if our children need us, and we have no energy left to give them?

It is true that we do not have the power to control what happens in the future, but we *can* control what we make of the present. Parents who take time to rest, when things are reasonably quiet, will have more than enough energy to face the storms that lie ahead.

What is merely beneficial to us now may, in the future, be the means to our survival. We should fortify ourselves as best we can, then brace ourselves for the days to come.

◆

I will try to nurture myself when I need it least, so that it sustains me when I need it most.

It is a good answer that knows when to stop.
—*Italian proverb*

Parents who give a long-winded answer to a simple question often find themselves being tuned out by their own children. We don't want to put our kids to sleep! We want to give answers that are age-appropriate and not any more or less than our children really need to know. A good answer stimulates your child to open another door, not to close the door for good.

If you keep your answers simple and to the point, you'll be sure to get the message across. If you make them eloquent and overstated, you may put up a barrier to future communication.

◆

It is my short and simple responses that my children are most receptive to; I will try not to be pontificating and long-winded.

Caged birds accept each other, but flight is what they long for.

—*Tennessee Williams*

Many of us unknowingly exercise a stranglehold on our children. We do not imprison them by exacting adherence to rules but rather by chaining them to our philosophies, binding them to our beliefs, making them slaves to our principles.

If we never give our children the chance to spread their wings, we may end up with parrots; they'll repeat exactly what they've heard us say, and will never have the ability to think for themselves.

They may accept us, even do tricks for us. But the truth is, the more we run their lives, the more desperate they'll be for a taste of freedom.

◆

I don't want my children to be "trained" into obedience. I want them to be able to think for themselves.

Never did we plan the morrow, for we had learned that in the wilderness some new and irresistible distraction is sure to turn up each day before breakfast.
—*Aldo Leopold*

Parents who do too much are overbooked, our weekdays jammed full of errands and activities, with no room left for spontaneity or surprise. If something comes up—some "irresistible distraction"—some unexpected fork in the road, we can't take advantage of it, because we fear that if we veer off our route even slightly, we may never find our way back.

Living by the calendar is a necessary evil, especially in these fast-paced times. But we should not be so overscheduled that we can't be lured away when something just happens to turn up. Our kids are as overcommitted as we force them to be, and with no time left to follow a whim or chase a shadow, their lives, too, may feel orchestrated and unspontaneous.

◆

I will try to leave some space on the calendar for the spontaneous and the unplanned.

Each day, and the living of it, has to be a conscious creation in which discipline and order are relieved with some play and some pure foolishness.

—*May Sarton*

We put order and discipline into our lives, so why do we feel guilty about putting "play" and "foolishness" into our lives as well?

When we choreograph our days, we ought to be thinking about scheduling time for pure fun—tennis or walking in the park or lunch with a friend or reading a good book. The calendar is almost too accommodating—expanding according to our commitments; if we don't schedule time for "play," if it isn't on the calendar, we will never find time for it.

We should not think of "free time" as a luxury. It is something we need, like a roof over our heads; not a gift, but a necessity.

◆

I won't feel guilty about planning free time for myself. From now on, I'll make sure to put it on the calendar.

Everything in life that we really accept undergoes a change.

—*Katherine Mansfield*

The key to enjoyment is acceptance. Embracing the task of parenting may be the means by which we grow.

Every day, we find ourselves surrounded by new obligations and duties, the expectations of our children and our spouses, the challenges of life. These do not usually come to us in blinding flashes. Rather, they are tiny nudges, little bursts of insight. We find ourselves wondering if we will be able to accommodate these changes, make the daily adjustments in our psyches that allow us to evolve as people and parents.

When we accept whatever comes, accept our role as parents, we find ourselves "becoming" what we never knew we could be. We leave our fears and doubts behind us and welcome all that is given to us and all that is asked of us.

◆

I am equal to this task. When I accept my role as a parent I grow into the job.

We have not the reverent feeling for the rainbow that the savage has, because we know how it is made. We have lost as much as we have gained by prying into the matter.

—*Mark Twain*

The overcommitted parent may want to instill an encyclopedia of knowledge into his child before she is three. When we do this, when we cram our children's minds with information, we may be taking away their innocent understanding of the world—their intuitive grasp of its beauty.

We forget how we came to know things—slowly, in our own good time. It is the uncovering of life, the unfolding of its treasures, that made us dance. When it is handed to us on a platter, demystified and distilled, it is nothing more than dime-store knowledge, worthless to us because it has already been decoded.

◆

I will not try to explain life to my children; I will do my best to expose them to it, then let it unfold for them slowly, in their own time.

Free to be you and me.

—*Marlo Thomas*

The freedom we give our children is not a gift—it is their right. We may have given them life, but we do not have the right to live it for them. Of course, we should offer them guidance, but we should never offer them a life plan; they need to develop one on their own.

If we are too hovering, too expectant, too demanding of our children, we may come dangerously close to driving them away from us. If we make them into clones of ourselves, we had better get used to looking in the mirror.

◆

I can see that my children and I are stronger as separate human beings than if we were to merge identities.

It seems to me that those songs that have been any good, I have nothing much to do with the writing of them. The words have just crawled down my sleeve and come out on the page.

—*Joan Baez*

Artists and musicians and writers know this: What is spontaneous, what we allow to come forward, pure and free, is the best part of us—our best art.

This also holds true for raising children. When we struggle as parents it is because we hold back when we instinctively ought to let go. Parenting is natural to us, if we only knew it. The days when we feel calm and free are the days when we do not fight what is natural—the days when we feel comfortable just letting go.

Each of us has a unique message we bring to our children—like a beautiful song or a brilliant watercolor—an expression of ourselves.

◆

Everyday I will give what is uniquely mine to give.

I love people. I love my family, my children...but inside myself is a place where I live all alone and that's where you renew your springs that never dry up.
—*Pearl S. Buck*

Buck was talking about a place we know well, even if we don't get there very often. It's a place where we feel comfortable, at peace. Here, there are no curiosity seekers, no critics. Here, we are never lonely; we are happily, blissfully alone. When we get to this place, we know we are safe and secure. There are no expectations, no demands on our time. We are home.

The springs may "never dry up"; still, we need to keep ourselves well watered. A once-a-day visit may be all that it takes to keep our spirits awake and alive.

◆

Inside myself is a place where I am free of the pressures and responsibilities of parenthood; today I will go there for a brief visit.

Likely as not, the child you can do least with will do the most to make you proud.

—*Mignon Mclaughlin*

We don't want to give up on our children. Still, there are times when we've tried it all—begging, pleading, threatening, punishing. Nothing works with this child, and we're not sure why.

We turn away and, bingo! Suddenly, magically, the child turns himself around. As if in response to our backing off, he finds a way to make it on his own. Despite all our concerns, he is the one who grows up and makes us proud.

Parents who do too much need to recognize when it is time just to let things run their course. What happens may surprise us. If we cannot set the course of change, we may be lucky enough to stand back and witness it.

◆

Sometimes I can be an effective parent by letting my children guide their own course.

At work, you think of the children you have left at home. At home. you think of the work you've left unfinished. Such a struggle is unleashed within yourself. Your heart is rent.

—*Golda Meir*

The dilemma of the modern parent: how to shift gears smoothly and efficiently. But we are not machines. We have a heart and it aches for what we leave behind.

There is help for this dilemma, and it comes through the art of transition. Whether it is through meditation or exercise or music, each of us must find a way to ease the pain of moving from one phase of our lives to another. Whether we don earphones and jog across town or listen to talk radio in rush hour traffic, each of us needs to find the most peaceful, comforting way to switch to another mode.

And we must accept the fact that this transition is never totally complete; we carry our children with us throughout the day, even if it is only in our hearts.

◆

When I shift abruptly from home to work and back again I cause myself a great deal of anxiety. I will find a way to create smoother transitions.

My ten-year old daughter is my number one power source.

—Hanan Mikhail Ashrawi

On this day, when things are not always what they seem—when little children masquerade as ghosts and goblins—we're reminded of how little we knew about children before we became parents.

We thought we would be the strong ones and our children would be weak and needy. Yet, our little ones, who now dance on the stage or move swiftly around the hockey arena, seem the picture of strength and fluidity, their confidence leaps and bounds ahead of our own.

This relationship I have with my children is not always what it appears to be. I am not always strong and sensible; they are not always weak and foolish.

◆

I take joy today in finding an unexpected source of strength. If it comes from my child, so much the better.

God, give us grace to accept with serenity the things that cannot be changed, courage to change the things which should be changed, and the wisdom to distinguish the one from the other.

—*Reinhold Niebuhr*

The serenity prayer, used daily by millions of people, is so simple, so beautifully stated, and so universally applicable that it's almost, at first reading, startling.

Parents who do too much don't know much about serenity. We get serenity mixed up with sleep, which most of us get enough of.

The serenity prayer is so important because it speaks to our need to control, our need to orchestrate what cannot be orchestrated, and the wisdom to know when to accept what cannot be changed.

◆

I will print the serenity prayer and hang it in a prominent place where I can refer to it often.

Love and skill together can create a miracle.
—*Anonymous*

Parents who do too much never really talk about or think about the skills that are necessary in parenting. Because no one goes to college to prepare to parent, and no one needs to pass a test to become a parent, there is obviously an enormous variance in the way we parent.

But if we bring our love to the act of parenting, our innate skills will surface. Love is the single most necessary element in gaining the "skill" of parenting. Loving our children is, in essence, what makes us parents.

Overcommitted parents may be too busy to show much love, or may show it in inappropriate ways. And, as for producing a "masterpiece"? Well, we need to do the best we can. After all, none of us is a "masterpiece"— that's for statues and paintings.

◆

If we bring love and empathy to the job of parenting, the skill will follow.

Some families are aware of the work addict's effect on them, yet feel very conflicted. Their conflict arises because the workaholic provides them with luxuries they would not ordinarily have. This is a typical bind for upwardly mobile workaholic families.

—*Diane Fassel*

It's very nice to live in a big house, with a swimming pool, in a great neighborhood, and belong to all the right clubs. But how did we come by this existence?

If we didn't inherit it, the chances are excellent that those who provided all of this are parents who did too much. And living the high life can be as addictive as creating the high life; and then you have an entire family co-dependent on overcommitted parents.

◆

I know the cost of providing what I thought my family wanted. Now I've come to realize, what they really want is a father and mother they can relate to, love, and trust.

Like that of many children of martyr parents, Julie's behavior alternated between two ineffective roles: rescuer and victim. Over the years she had attempted to become her mother's friend, therapist, adviser and...adopted parent.

—*Harold H. Bloomfield*

When we overextend ourselves we often become martyr parents. We force our children to adapt to our crazy, obsessive patterns of behavior. Because we are not dependable or consistent, we unknowingly place our children in the role of confidants, enablers, co-conspirators, and, finally, victims.

It is a kind of abusive relationship—that of being a martyr parent. What child can live up to our expectations, our demands, our inconsistent parenting? Parents who do too much are often *destructive* exactly when they think they're being *constructive*.

◆

Nobody trusts or respects a martyr. But children, because they are dependent, need to fit into our upside-down world. I think it would be wise to put myself in my child's place, especially when we are locked in battle.

In every cry of every man,
In every infant's cry of fear,
In every voice, in every ban,
The mind-forged manacles I hear.

—*William Blake*

Overcommitted parents are often fearful people who need to invent rules and regulations that stifle the emotional and creative growth of their children.

When we curb freedom and make the concept of it a privilege rather than a right, we begin to imprison our children and ourselves in a web of self-doubt, deceit, distrust, and anger.

In an attempt to mold our children, we often stunt their growth, cheating them out of their creative liberty and other means of self-expression. Most likely, we do this out of fear.

◆

When I restrict myself, I restrict my children. No garden ever grew by sheer force of will.

The important thing is not so much that every child should be taught, as that every child should be given the wish to learn.

—*John Lubbock*

In our haste we may make assumptions about our children, many of which turn out to be inaccurate.

For example, our push to "educate" our children, to make sure that they are near or at the top of their class, we may be creating young people who find the act of learning totally displeasing—a task that is completed for the sake of itself. The means become the object, the end superfluous.

We need to help instill in our children the fun of learning, the pure joy in finding out about our world, discovering their true interests and talents. When they are driven to perform and excel, they may mistrust the parent and loathe the classroom.

◆

There may be more to be learned sitting in a sandbox with a pail and shovel than reciting the answers from some tired, obsolete textbook.

Whether we are together or apart, each of us is whole. We may be of one, but not one together.

—*Anonymous*

Parents who are too heavily invested in their children are often people who feel that their kids are only extensions of them.

One example of this is when we define our children by trying to figure out which parent they take after. Not that there's anything wrong with genetics, but maybe we ought to question our need to constantly describe our children in terms of ourselves.

We have, of course, common experiences throughout life; but we must ensure that our children feel, at least to some degree, unique in how they perceive themselves and their world.

◆

Yes, my children are of me, but not for me. I will not define them as I define myself.

One touch is worth ten thousand words.
> —*Harold Bloomfield, Melba Cosgrove,*
> *and Peter McWilliams*

Some of us parents were not shown or given much physical evidence of love or tenderness by our parents. When we are aloof and "untouchable" we become even more distant, more detached from our children.

There are times when words will not do; we may have a speech ready to give, but the tenderness of a parent's hand on the shoulder, or a hug and a kiss on the weary forehead of a disappointed child really says it all.

We do not need to verbalize everything we want or need to say.

◆

Parents who do too much usually talk too much. There is purity and forgiveness in the act of silent touch.

There ain't nothin' wrong with young people. Jus' quit lyin' to em.'

—"Moms" Mabley

We don't mean to lie to them. Or most of the time we don't. The problem is that we want a perfect world, a perfect home, and a perfect school for our children. Because perfection does not exist in these places, we lie to our children, with the best of intentions.

Then, when our children are disappointed to discover the truth—that all of us are fallible and imperfect— they lose their respect for us. Our lies were meant to cushion the blows of reality, but they become a setup and an invitation to mistrust.

◆

I do not want to burden my children with the bare facts and inequities and atrocities that take place in life. I do want to respect them enough to introduce these realities as long as they are ready to hear them.

He knew the precise psychological moment when to say nothing.

—*Oscar Wilde*

Silence is often called for, especially when we are in an argument with our children or our spouse. But parents who do too much do not know the value of silence—of allowing time to pass between edicts, directions, and accusations.

We need to be better students of nuance, of how and when to talk to one another. Often we're so caught up in managing the kids that we find ourselves hoarse from speaking, tired from our obsessive oration, and, frankly, our children tire of it before we do.

◆

It takes restraint and sensitivity to know when to be silent.

Little things affect little minds.

—*Benjamin Disraeli*

We need to be magnanimous in our reception to ideas, especially those that come from our children. Just because our thirteen-year-old son buys a heavy metal CD to play on the stereo does not mean he's also a drug runner and a cocaine addict.

If each difference of opinion and every unpleasant comment from our children throws us into a tailspin— if we treat every event with the same gravity—we are overly invested in our parenting. Every single word, every negative thought, need not be weighed and reacted to.

◆

There are graver problems just ahead. Today I want to make sure I don't sweat the small stuff.

Liberty is the only thing you can't have unless you give it to others.

—*William Allen White*

Giving our children the freedom to grow, to have first-hand experience at winning and losing is important; but liberty is also a great teacher and can offer more to our children than a thousand lectures or a hundred punishments.

We want freedom for ourselves, too. What we don't realize is that we are imprisoned by the control we exercise over our children. When we expect too much, when we try to make our child's world a perfect one—we are chained to the elaborate vision we've set forth, bound to our unwavering commitment to our child's destiny.

Freedom doesn't mean lack of parenting or supervision, but it does mean knowing when to allow our children the liberty they need in order to grow. When we lock in a set of expectations, we are also imprisoned by them.

◆

If I am convinced that I am unworthy of liberty, how can I pass along any different message to my children?

"Parents Overboard"
—*Sign hung in the rear window of a VW bus in Los Angeles*

Perhaps the sign was handmade, but if it were mass-produced, it would probably sell in the thousands.

Parents who do too much are often "overboard." In trying too hard we drown in a sea of our own making.

Children who learn self-sufficiency and independence don't have "overboard" parents. Self-reliance has never been passed on by a parent who is hypervigilant, wanting to control every aspect of a child's life.

❖

There is room for spontaneity, freedom, and self-actualization. But we must give our children the room they need to attain it.

One of the unhappiest stages on the way to adulthood is losing the baby fat of naiveté that had us believing that everyone on earth is a wonderful human being with our best interests at heart.

—*Harvey Mackay*

It is a hard lesson to learn, especially when you're the child whose parents sheltered you too much.

Parents who are overprotective may inadvertently create dependent situations by not giving their children adequate preparation for the realities of how the world and its people interact.

While it would be upsetting and disheartening to constantly warn our children of the wolves out there, we need to do our best to strike a balance when it comes to explaining that there are people whose values are not like our own, and who may be dishonest and threatening.

◆

Too much negative opinion can make an enthusiastic and open child into a wary, doubting, and small-minded adult. But we must parcel out the realities of the world so our children will not be shocked back into the nest.

The closed mind, if closed long enough, can be opened by nothing short of dynamite.

—*Gerald W. Johnson*

Intractability is the curse of the overcommitted parent. We are too often too sure. We do not question our parenting methods, and we're rarely open to self-examination.

Being certain—never questioning—makes us closed parents. We need to be as curious about the world and the way it works as we want our children to be.

Inflexibility is not an asset. When we are highly opinionated, we do not give our children any doors to open; instead, we pass along to them a highly prescribed, closed outlook on life.

◆

We need to limber up, do some mind-stretching exercises, listen to opinions other than our own, and keep the doors and windows open so our children get the fresh air of an open mind.

I told the kids in Taos High School that day to trust in what they loved, that you don't know where it will lead you. The important thing is to love something, even if it's skateboarding or car mechanics or whistling. Let yourself love it completely.

—*Natalie Goldberg*

As parents, we need to *allow* them to love it completely. If our child wants to pump gas for a living, our only restriction is this: that he be happy doing it, not *resigned* to it.

We cannot control our children's interests, their hobbies, their obsessions-*du-jour*. We need to engender in them the passion to follow their muse. Not every child goes to Harvard, becomes a corporate executive, and, in later life, supports his parents in the manner to which they've aspired.

◆

We know, as adults, what was in our hearts, what we really wanted as children. We also know how those dreams were thwarted and stunted.

My father had faith in me and loved me. Maybe you don't exactly learn from that, but it allows you to take on the world. I grew up knowing I was accepted and loved, and that made an incredible difference.

—*Bernie Siegel*

Only open arms can cradle a child and his dreams.

If we believe that, among other things we learned from our mothers and fathers, they deeply and truly loved us, we have the courage to face the world. To know you are accepted—this is the bottom line for most children.

Parents who do too much are often too judgmental, too afraid to let life "happen." We are busy building a house of cards called expectation, held together by ridiculous demands.

If we end up leaving our children with only one thing, it must be unconditional love.

◆

I believe my children will learn from having a parent who trusts and loves them.

> Other people have discovered useful alibis in their developmental histories. I was neglected as a child . . . I am the child of an alcoholic . . . my father deserted me . . . and so on.
> —*Gayle Rosellini and Mark Worden*

We're all victims of various kinds of mistakes in parenting. All of us have a story to tell or a complaint to air.

What we must make certain not to do is arrange our stories as "alibis" for our children—so that we (and they) can rationalize their inappropriate behaviors.

The mirror shows all of us the same image: our face. And we must face up to our upbringings, the mistakes and unhappiness we had as children—and get beyond them. Only then can we have a clean enough slate not to repeat what was "done" to us, and not foist the same behaviors and attitudes on our children, and they, in turn, on their children.

◆

It's not enough to name the disease. I must do everything I can to conquer it. My child's life depends on it.

Each generation imagines itself to be more intelligent than the one that went before it, and wiser than the one that comes after it.

—*George Orwell*

Why is it assured that because your fourteen-year old has just discovered a universal truth, henceforth everything he thinks and everything he does is greater, grander, and more on-target than what you, his parents, experienced?

Perhaps this is just one of youth's prerogatives—and we must learn to be patient with it. Our children are discovering life's wonders, and whether it be the Beatles, Clint Black, or the Red Hot Chili Peppers, it is their world and we need to let them make their home in it.

◆

I will try to remember what I was like as a kid—when I automatically assumed that my parents were not up on things—and because I knew about popular culture and a bit of psychology, I was way beyond them.

Habit, if not resisted, soon becomes necessity.
—*Saint Augustine*

What we do daily is what we become. If we are courageous, we become brave. If we are fearful, we become afraid. And, if our lives are lived only for the external reward, we become addicted to that reward—so much so that looking inward, or toward our homes and families, is considered secondary.

We have to be careful of our habits. They mold us and shape us and lure us onto a foreign landscape that soon becomes familiar terrain. They are traps of our own making that become as easy for us to accept as they were once hard to initiate.

What we do habitually is so familiar that we forget to question its authenticity—its relationship to our beliefs. We are what we do—and, as parents who do too much, we must be ever so careful about the way we spend our time.

◆

I must reevaluate my daily life to see whether my habits are overshadowing my needs.

Many persons have a wrong idea of what constitutes true happiness. It is not attained through self-gratification but through fidelity to a worthy purpose.

—*Helen Keller*

As parents who do too much, we know that what really makes us happy is to be certain that our children are happy. But we often get things mixed up—we may seek our own self-gratification by furnishing our children with things. We feel like the best parents because our kids have all the right toys—the newest computer, the newest video games, and so on.

What makes us whole as parents is the love and security we provide. That is and always will be the best kind of self-gratification.

◆

"When you're happy, I'm happy." We needn't be obsessed to find joy in parenting happy children.

Children reinvent your world for you.
—*Susan Sarandon*

Everyone says it, and it's true. When we have our first child, our entire lives change in ways we never imagined they would. This new world we have before us can baffle us, frighten us, and demand things of us that we don't know if we can deliver.

If we feel burdened by these changes, and resent the ways in which we are forced to redirect our lives, we may be setting the foundation for future difficulties. In order to compensate for these feelings of intrusion, we may turn into rigid and inflexible parents. It sounds like a paradox and it is: When we feel "strangled" by the demands of new parenthood, we may react by being overly attentive and overcommitted to our children.

◆

I need to be open to the changes that are brought about by parenthood. Reinvention does not necessarily mean loss of self.

I didn't realize how much I would learn from my children. They have shown me there are more important things than planning and organizing. They've given me more humanity.

—*Joanne Quillen*

Parenting more with our hearts, less with our heads or our pocketbooks, gives us the freedom to learn as we grow with our children.

Overcommitted parents rarely do anything spontaneously. We predict. We plan. We overorchestrate every hour of the day and night, rarely allowing for chance. Being open to change and flexible enough not to be derailed by the unexpected does spring us from our self-induced prisons, giving way to the humanity of inconsistency and surprise.

◆

Allowing for change and making a place for it in your home is an act of giving.

Children find comfort in flaws, ignorance, insecurities similar to their own. I love my mother for letting me see hers.

—*Erma Bombeck*

When we're honest with our children, we let them see us as we are. If we present to them the pretense of perfection and an image that's unattainable, we set our children up for defeat.

We don't stop loving our children because they failed a math test or because they turned their CD players up so loud they could be heard on Mars. And they won't stop loving us because we ran out of gas on the freeway or forgot to pick them up after baseball practice.

Our children need to see our faults and our foibles, to see us in error and in good humor. They need to know that we're people—and that we're approachable and imperfect.

◆

I know my children will forgive my imperfections if I give them a chance to see them up close.

Instant gratification takes too long.

—*Carrie Fisher*

Parents who do too much do too many things at the same time. We've all seen evidence of this, or maybe this scene will remind you of your family:

A mother and father in a shopping mall with their children. Each child is holding an ice cream cone and a balloon, and clutching a bag of popcorn.

Or this: a similar family at the city zoo. It's not enough that they're there to see the animals—they also have cotton candy and hot dogs; one of them is listening to a Walkman; the father is reading the sports pages of the newspaper while pushing the stroller.

We need every possible gratification—and we need it instantly. Hungry? Just get something to eat while you're going through the monkey house. Need a soundtrack while you're watching the dolphins? Just crank up the portable tape player.

◆

I can't teach my children appropriate lessons in patience if I need to have my own needs met instantaneously.

Auntie Em: Hate you. Hate Kansas. Taking dog.
Dorothy

—*Anonymous*

Haven't all of us wanted to run away from home at least once in our lives?

As our children grow older, they need to be allowed certain liberties. Parents who do too much often hold on to their children and stifle, unknowingly, the growth of self-dependence their children pursue.

We must not be too confining in our love—we need to face the fact that soon we will see our children grow into adulthood. To do this, they need a gentle and steady hand, guidance and encouragement, not a tightening of the reins. If we are willing to supply to them the self-esteem and independence they need, they'll grow happily and confidently upward.

◆

During those times that it is crucial for my children to show their independence and exercise their free will, I need to step back and not always try to control their destinies.

There's nothing so unequal as the equal treatment of unequals. Individualize your leadership.

—*Anonymous*

Often children complain that they pay for the sins of their siblings. We sometimes dole out blanket punishments—expect the same level of "good behavior" from each of our children and ignore their profound differences, their strengths as well as their weaknesses.

If we take the time to listen to our children, observe their interests and idiosyncrasies, and become sensitive to their uniqueness, then we can tailor our expectations to each child.

Democracy, when carried to an extreme, is tyranny.

◆

One child may be emotionally needy, the other self-assured and independent. A third may have astonishing talents that need to be nurtured. It seems obvious, but I do need to be aware of my children's differences.

Life isn't a matter of milestones, but of moments.
—*Rose Fitzgerald Kennedy*

Every time parent groups get together, whether it's a school open house, a church potluck, or a Saturday morning soccer match, there's always a lively exchange about one another's children.

But listen closely to what is said. We talk about our children in terms of their "milestones." "Yes, Michael's now in the seventh grade and in honors math." "Our Ross has just won the fourth-grade spelling bee, and he's on the school swimming team." "Abigail has learned all the lines for her lead in the school play."

Of course we should be proud of our kids' accomplishments. But it might be better if we heard other kinds of exchanges: "Ross asked me last night if Mom was my best friend." "Abigail said she wanted to make a special day for me on Saturday because I've been working so hard." "Michael spent his afternoon making a 'welcome home' sign for his dad today."

◆

If I could remember, and learn to record those "moments," I could look back at the essence of my days with my children. I can always look at their report cards for the milestones.

After all, tomorrow is another day.
—*Margaret Mitchell*

Parents who do too much get caught up in the finality of decisions. At the end of each day we secretly rate what we've done: "Have I been too strict?" "Was I right in being honest about my child's friends?" "Did I do irreparable damage when I grounded our sixteen-year old?"

We must learn that forgiveness and flexibility are two of the cornerstones of healthy parenting. Tomorrow is another day—a chance for renewal. To say "I'm sorry, I was wrong" or "I must stand by my opinion."

We are inflexible in our decision-making, but later, we always doubt ourselves.

◆

Life is about change. I may reconsider my decisions or methods of parenting when I need to.

The willingness to accept responsibility for one's own life is the source from which self-respect springs.
—*Joan Didion*

When we are accountable for what we do and what we say, and our children see us illustrate that accountability, it is a gift we give them.

Self-respect and confidence are born of acceptance. Only when we dance through life, like a bull at the ballet, with no regard for who we hurt or the damage we do, do we foster children who take no responsibility for their actions. And when children see no correlation between action and result, they never need to learn accountability or self-respect.

◆

I do not want to raise children who get in the "blame" rut—children who do not know how to look within. I want my children to say "This is my life, and I am responsible for the way I live it."

In my room as a kid, I used to create an atmosphere
of the ring; I'd play a fighter and get knocked to the
floor and come back to win.

—*Dustin Hoffman*

We're eager to let our children in on the "secrets of
life"—to turn them into pragmatists and realists. We
must take care not to destroy their fantasies too young,
to leap too quickly to deliver the truth, and burst the
bubble of their youth.

Whether they're with an imaginary friend or just play-
acting, our children are learning about life in their
own way, preparing themselves for the "real thing" by
fighting bad guys and launching imaginary rockets in
their dreams. Like Dorothy in *The Wizard of Oz,* they
learn about greed and evil by surviving it in the land of
their dreams.

◆

If my child does not always let me into his world it is be-
cause he is preparing to someday enter mine.

December 2

> We never talked, my family. We communicated by putting Ann Landers articles on the refrigerator.
>
> —*Judy Gold*

The modern family. We communicate in strange ways: Post-it notes and cellular phones; writing on fogged mirrors and leaving a trail of telltale cookie crumbs. Somehow or other, we let each other know what we're up to. We've come a long way since smoke signals. Or have we?

With all the modern gadgetry, are we actually engaged in "better" forms of communication? Or do we just reach each other "faster?" Perhaps we tune into our child's whereabouts, yet know next-to-nothing about what she's thinking. What she's "up to" isn't necessarily what she's "into."

If we want to really know our children—and, likewise, let our children know us—we need to arrange more intimate forms of communication. We need to talk to one another, not just use the latest high-tech form of "communication."

◆

I know where my children are, but I may not always know what they're thinking. Today I'll try to arrange time for a talk.

I not only bow to the inevitable; I am fortified by it.
—*Thornton Wilder*

If we are honest with ourselves, we have to admit that what is "inevitable" isn't worth worrying about. What we cannot control, what is beyond our powers or the powers of any man or woman, we are better off embracing.

To embrace the unknown, to be "fortified" by it, we have to learn to let go. Whether we are clinging to some worn-out notion of the past, or to some crazy, impossible vision for the future, we need to replace it with the one thing we do have: acceptance.

What I accept is suddenly within my control, because I admit that I am powerless to change it. Acceptance is possibly the most liberating characteristic a parent can possess. It gives us the freedom to walk toward the future without shame or fear.

◆

When I accept the inevitable, I also embrace the possible.

A sobering thought: What if, right at this very moment, I *am* living up to my full potential?

—*Jane Wagner*

Parents who do too much may be constantly looking toward the future, caught up in the dream that there is always something better—just over the next hill: a bigger house, a faster car, a better school for the children.

But what is here and now, what is right before us, is the thing we must pay attention to. Don't we realize that all that we have—right now, right at this very moment—may be all that we ever need?

Pinning all our hopes and dreams on the future is a bit like putting our life savings into a slot machine. It may turn out okay, but is it really worth the gamble?

◆

I will place more of my energy on the here and now. I may not have all I want, but I may have all I need.

Her little girl was late arriving home from school, so the mother asked her why:

"I had to help another girl. She was in trouble," replied the daughter.

"What did you do to help her?"

"Oh, I sat down and helped her cry."

—*Anonymous*

Parents who do too much often try to be "fixers." We think that by solving our children's problems, we are being good, caring parents.

We forget that it's impossible to ease the pain of another human being, even our own child, no matter how hard we try. The best we can do, and sometimes it's a lot, is sit beside them, hold their hand, and "help them cry."

◆

My children need support more than they need solutions.

December 6

War is the unfolding of miscalculations.
—*Barbara Tuchman*

Parents, especially parents of teenagers, can learn valuable lessons from the history books.

Miscues, miscommunications, crossed signals all lead to mounting tensions and finally to full-scale war, not just on the battlefield, but right in our own homes. When rules and regulations become a substitute for trust, when they replace real communication, we are in danger of inciting a riot.

Of course our children need limits. But they also need to know that we value their integrity and trust their judgment. Without trust, (whether it is between nations or between parent and child) there is little chance for honest communication, and without communication there is little chance of achieving a lasting peace.

◆

I'd rather my children were my allies than my enemies; communication may be my best hope.

When your schedule leaves you brain-drained and stressed to exhaustion, it's time to give up something. Delegate. Say no. Be brutal. It's like cleaning out a closet—after a while it gets easier to get rid of things. You discover that you really didn't need them anyway.
—*Marilyn Ruman*

Our lives and our closets have a lot in common. Both are cluttered with things we could easily do without.

Why, then, do we put up with these crazy schedules, these days of perpetual motion? Perhaps it is because we want to shield ourselves from the fear of loneliness, of emptiness. We think that if our lives are full, they are also full of meaning.

The truth is, we are sentenced by our calendars to a life of nonstop "production," and we are having trouble connecting with our families and ourselves. We may be busy, but we're no longer sure *why* we're busy.

◆

I need some time for quiet reflection. If I'm "unproductive" for an hour or two, I may learn something valuable.

My old father used to have a saying: if you make a bad bargain, hug it all the tighter.

—*Abraham Lincoln*

When we're out chasing rainbows, sometimes we have to run through the rain.

Those of us who are parents of "exceptional" children have a slightly different route to follow from other parents, one that requires near superhuman strength and an amazing amount of flexibility and patience and hope. We definitely feel that we have more than we bargained for.

If we have a child with learning disabilities or physical handicaps, he may need us to hug him all the tighter, yet also need us to be able to let go. This is a balancing act—and, for those parents who go through it daily, a near-impossible task.

◆

It helps to realize that none of us enter parenthood with a script. I know I am improvising as I go along, learning my "lines" as I speak them.

We awaken in others the same attitude of mind we hold toward them.

—*Elbert Hubbard*

If we are martyrs, we awaken "martyrdom" in our children. If we see parenthood as a "duty" and do our best to accommodate our children, no matter what the cost to ourselves, we turn our children into the same self-sacrificing adults.

The object of parenthood is not self-sacrifice. We can give to our children without stripping ourselves naked. We don't end up better for that and neither do they. In the end, all of us come to realize that martyrdom is nothing more than an elaborate cover-up, a method of controlling what we most fear.

What we do now, the choices we make for ourselves are the legacy we give to our children. If we want them to be healthy, self-confident adults, the best we can do is pass on our own state of well-being.

◆

When I take care of myself, I provide for my children's future.

I'd gone through life believing in the strength and competences of others; never in my own. Now, dazzled, I discovered that *my* capacities were real. It was like finding a fortune in the lining of an old coat.

—*Joan Mills*

This is what parenting can do for us: It can be a remarkable journey toward self-discovery, a time when we learn that we are actually more and better than we ever knew. That is, if we trust ourselves and let our instincts take over.

When we become parents we should think of it as the greatest adventure of our lives—a time when we can be uniquely confident in our own skills and abilities. This is not a time to look around; it's a time to look inside. Get to know the person you were meant to be and unveil the contribution that is yours to make.

If we do this, we'll experience a high we've never known before. It does not come from power or even from a sense of accomplishment—it comes from the connection we make with a place deep inside ourselves.

◆

Finding my own source of strength and learning that it is of great value makes me feel lighter than ever.

I long to put the experience of fifty years at once into your young lives, to give you at once the key of that treasure chamber every gem of which has cost me tears and struggles and prayers, but you must work for these inward treasures yourselves.

—*Harriet Beecher Stowe*

What parent hasn't felt this way? It would be so much easier to "transfer" than to guide. If we could just pour ourselves into our children, hand over to them what it has taken us years to learn, how wonderful that would be.

Wonderful, but destructive. For when we do too much for our children, when we try to give them *our* lessons, to convey to them the results of *our* struggles, we are like the magician who tells his audience beforehand how he pulls the rabbit out of the hat. We're not only destroying the illusion, we're cheating them out of their sense of wonder, their chance to unravel the mystery of their own lives.

◆

If I give too much, my children have no chance to struggle, to find their own "inward treasures."

A man travels the world over in search of what he needs and returns home to find it.

—*George Moore*

How do we define success? Is it a trophy? Is it how we look in a new Armani suit? Is it a year-end bonus? Or is it something intangible, something we can feel but we can't explain?

The key phrase in Moore's insightful quote is "what he needs." When we try to satisfy our needs rather than our wants, we connect with that intangible thing called success. When we try to satisfy our wants, we may look the image of success but feel empty inside.

To satisfy our needs, we may need to go no further than our own families, our homes, our children. Once we have our "needs" taken care of, we will attach far less importance to our "wants."

◆

I may be looking for success in all the wrong places. Perhaps it is right in front of my eyes and always has been.

If I were given the choice, to accept the experience, with everything that it entails, or to refuse the bitter largesse, I would have to stretch out my hands—because out of it has come, for all of us, an unimagined life.

—*Clara Claiborne Park*

Park was writing about the joy that came to her through the pain of raising an autistic child. Still, her words apply to all of us—all of us who are in this business of raising children.

For none of us knows what lies ahead for our children. And if we *were* told of future problems—the heartaches, the struggles, and the disappointments—there aren't many of us who wouldn't do as Park suggests, "stretch out [our] hands" to take what was offered.

◆

Parenthood runs the gamut of life's experiences—the good and the bad, the painful and the joyous. I will try to accept them all, as they come.

December 14

If you can do it then why do it?

—Gertrude Stein

Most of us rise to the challenges of life. We do things on a dare and on impulse. We jump into the burning building, even if we're not sure we'll come out. We take incredible chances and often live close to the edge.

Parenthood is the biggest chance we'll ever take. We jump into it without knowing very much about it. It's a high-stakes game, and we're in it for life. But after all, if we knew we could do it, why do it? It's the challenge of parenting that's exciting—the unique chance to create a life and watch it unfold.

Although we may not know it at the outset, parenthood is not only our greatest challenge; it is also our greatest adventure.

◆

I have the spirit of a pioneer, and the soul of a parent.

It's not so much how busy you are, but why you are busy. The bee is praised; the mosquito is swatted.
—*Marie O'Conner*

The trouble comes when "busy" becomes an excuse. "I can't play a game of cards because I'm busy." "I can't watch your ballet practice because I'm busy." "I can't go with you on the field trip because I'm busy."

Okay, some of this "busyness" is legitimate and acceptable and even productive. You really do have important things to do. You can't always be where your children want you to be—and you shouldn't. But is there one moment out of your busy day that could be put on hold? Is there an appointment you could reschedule, an errand you could overlook?

When our "busyness" becomes a mask that we hide behind—perhaps unconsciously, but nevertheless destructively—we need to look closely at that fast track we're on. We may be busy like a mosquito, droning around and around in circles.

◆

I want to be busy if I'm productive; I don't want to flit about from one thing to another, unable to commit myself to any part of my life.

Fear is a question. What are you afraid of and why?
Our fears are a treasure house of self-knowledge if we
explore them.

—*Marilyn French*

One of the most damaging and growth-stunting things
we can portray to our children is a lack of fear. We're
not talking about the ghosts in the attic, but we *are*
talking about the fear of getting close to friends, of
trusting one's instincts, of trying things for the first
time.

Parents who do too much may be too busy to allow
their children into their private world—a world where
fear is often the catalyst for courage. We must realize
that empathy is a powerful tool. If we admit our fears
to our children, we become human and welcoming to
them.

We need to create an atmosphere where self-examination is welcomed—where we let our children know
that we, too, have fears. When we do this, we show our
children that self-knowledge is a fascinating landscape
that helps break down the power of fear.

◆

*I will try not to hide my fear from my children. If I show
myself only to be stoic, I present them with impossible standards and roadblocks to growth and self-confidence.*

A man with a watch knows what time it is; a man with two watches isn't so sure.

—*Anonymous*

When we have more than one master, it's difficult to know which way to go. As parents who do too much, we are often confused by the abundance of advice that comes from every direction.

We get such mixed signals, such disparate views, that we are often left in a daze. Fearful of making the wrong decision, we're unable to make *any* decision regarding our children, and we end up secretly hoping the problem, whatever it is, will just disappear.

We need to learn how to distill the information that comes to us from every phone call, book, TV channel, friend, teacher or in-law. These "voices" all have an opinion—theirs. With so many divergent points of view, we should realize that there is no right or wrong answer. There is only *our* answer—the one voice, the one master we should follow.

◆

Whether or not I am pointed in the right direction, I am sure it is the only direction that will lead me—and my children—to a comfortable place.

Ultimately, love is self-approval.

—*Sondra Ray*

We've heard this before, but need to be reminded. If we cannot love ourselves, at least on some level, we cannot give love.

And we must "approve" of ourselves if we are to "approve" of our children. When we are at our self-deprecating worst, we tend to be less nurturing, more superficial in our parenting.

As parents who do too much, we need to learn how to live life less externally and look within for answers, approval, or direction. Only then can we be generous and nonjudgmental in our assessment of our children.

It's true: We can't give it if we don't have it.

◆

I want to be inner-directed, and approve of myself for who I am and how I parent.

People fighting their aloneness will do almost anything to avoid silence.

—*Myrtle Barber*

You know the type. Maybe you are the type. People who cannot be alone. They seek out public places to be near people. They vacation at crowded beaches and resorts. They are on one committee after another. They donate their time. They cannot be home alone.

Being alone, the house silent, is anathema to those parents who are fearful and resistant to self-examination. They've camouflaged their loneliness by being around people all the time. At night, they're on the phone; the next morning they make sure to get out of the house as soon as possible.

Silence invites us to be introspective. It challenges us to go within, to confront our fears and examine our dreams. This is not a lonely place, but one that makes us look into the mirror. If we avoid the reflection, we avoid life.

◆

While I do not want to be self-obsessed, I do want to be introspective enough to be a participant in my life and in the lives of my children.

Healthy relationships imply supporting each other, yet there is no focus upon "fixing" the other person. Each person's process is respected and it is recognized that each must do what he or she must.

—*Anne Wilson Schaef*

Parents who do too much always do too much "fixing" the kids. Somehow we think, without admitting it, that there is only *one* way to do something, to be somebody, to react to pain, to attain goals, to suffer hardships, to bring up our children.

Each person has his own rate of living, his own ability, or lack of it, to learn. Each person reacts to opposition or negativity in his own way. Each person's process of growth is different from the next.

We often remark on how different our children are—their temperaments, their humor, their talents and interests. Of course they're different—they are, after all, two or three or four different human beings.

◆

I do not want to "fix" my children or attempt to create them in either my image or the currently popular image of "perfect" children. I know it will only lead to unhappiness, disappointment, and, finally, alienation.

Remember, when they have a tantrum, don't have one of your own.

—*Judith Kuriansky*

We've all been guilty of it. When we're exhausted, it's the end of the day, and we've been as patient as Job, we finally hit the roof, unable to conjure up one more ounce of understanding.

So when our beautiful three-year-old daughter turns into something resembling Linda Blair in *The Exorcist*, we snap—and begin bellowing louder than she is doing, commanding her to shut up and sit down in the stroller and saying, "No, you cannot have another cupcake!"

Here's a better way to calm the waters: When your child becomes inconsolable, insolent, and begins a full-fledged tantrum, try to speak evenly, quietly, looking her straight in the eye, and hugging her. Believe it or not, it will disarm both of you most of the time. And there is no better cure for anger and frustration than the demonstration of love.

◆

Giving in to your children can be nearly as damaging as imitating their behavior. I will try, instead, to deflect my anger with love and evenness.

My mother once defined me as "someone who never has an unexpressed thought." She gave me what I've always considered excellent advice when she said, "There is a difference between telling the truth and telling everything you know."

—*Kathryn Carpenter*

How many times have we said "The truth hurts"? The truth can be told in ways that is less lethal to the one who is about to be hurt by it.

If we must criticize our children—the way they dress, comb their hair, the friends they choose—there are so many ways not to hurt them and shame them in the process.

Does your daughter try too hard to imitate Madonna? Don't make her feel bad by belittling her idol or her looks. Suggest a different kind of makeup; help her discover how she might develop her own look.

There are so many ways to tell the truth to your children; demoralizing them isn't one.

◆

Sometimes less is more, in the truth department. The whole unvarnished truth may do nothing but destroy a child's self-esteem. A carefully and lovingly told truth can be constructive and affirming.

These are my daughters, I suppose. But where in the world did the children vanish?

—*Phyllis McGinley*

How do we treat our children after they've become adults? The test of parents who do too much continues. Do we immerse ourselves in their trials and tribulations? Do we begin to overparent our grandchildren?

Some of us are overboard in the ways we continue to parent our adult children. We say, "He'll always be my little boy," or, "She never could make up her mind, even when she was just a toddler."

We must begin to see our children as our peers. It is not easy. We know them intimately and have been part of their lives for decades. But now they are adults and no longer need the same things from us that they once did. The trick for us is not to need the same things from them that we once did.

◆

I like who my children have become. I want to be open to these changes.

One generation plants the trees; another gets the shade.

—*Chinese proverb*

Investing in our children with time, love, understanding, and openness is all we really have. We cannot resent our children for taking advantage of what we freely give.

One of the most often heard phrases begins "When I was your age…" (fill in the blank). So many of us remind our children of how good they have it, how much they have, and how much better life is for them than it was for us.

Well, why do we provide so well for our children? Why do we give them the thing we never had?

But we must be careful, because too much shade may make a cool place to lie in, but it may also make a bad place to grow the trees that we plant.

◆

Perhaps each successive generation does a little better than the last—they are healthier and have better lives—because each generation behind them remembered to plant those trees.

We can do no great things—only small things with great love.

—Mother Teresa

Parents who do too much tend to be grandiose in terms of their expectations—of themselves *and* of their children.

We put so much energy, so much hope behind our children (which is, of course, a setup), that we expect great things from them and from ourselves.

Small kindnesses, moments of quiet time, walks in the autumn leaves and the winter snow, translate to to our children as precious moments conveyed with love.

We do not remember the grand gifts, the much trumpeted acts of giving by our parents as much as we do the times they read to us, the camping trip with Dad, or the moments of quiet conversation. Those are the small things that are infused with love.

◆

What our children really want from us is really so easy to give—our time, our attention. It is the small things that carry great weight.

There are people who put their dreams in a little box and say, "Yes, I've got dreams, of course, I've got dreams." Then they put the box away and bring it out once in a while to look in it, and yep, they're still there. These are *great* dreams, but they never even get out of the box. It takes an uncommon amount of guts to put your dreams on the line, to hold them up and say, "How good or bad am I?" That's where the courage comes in.

—*Erma Bombeck*

When we hold our dreams at bay, putting them off in order to raise the family, we become martyrs. We need to find time for our dreams—to become whole people, and better parents.

It takes courage and conviction to pursue our ideals. We cannot fall into the easy excuse that "being a parent is a full-time job," and that we have no time for our own interests.

◆

If I allow myself to pursue some of my dreams, I will be a more fully realized person—and parent.

I seem to have an awful lot of people inside me.
—*Dame Edith Evans*

And all of then are giving mixed messages and plenty of conflicting advice. Sometimes all of this advice derails our thinking. We know what's "right," but we have an unharmonious Greek chorus in our heads that causes us confusion.

We need to trust ourselves and our first decisions more often. Too much "advice," whether well-intentioned or merely meddlesome, tends to cloud our judgment and make us doubt our every thought.

We are so many people. We are a composite of our mothers and our fathers, our teachers and our coaches and our priests and our rabbis. But with all that input, we still don't have all the answers, even if our children think we do and expect us to.

◆

It is important that I observe my "inner factions"—but it is dangerous to allow too many outside voices to rule my heart.

You can't saw sawdust.

—*Harvey Mackay*

Those of us who are overcommitted tend to beat the dead horse. When a decision has been made, by our children or by ourselves, even if it is a poor choice, a mistake in judgment, we need to move on, to let go.

Obsessive talk does not revise history. We sometimes talk ourselves into a historical rewrite of sorts—retell the story long enough and after a while it bears little resemblance to reality.

We need to learn which things we can walk away from and chalk up to experience and which things we really need to reflect on, to rethink and discuss, in order to learn from our mistakes.

◆

The value of reflection is great, but obsessive reflection is pointless; it saps our energy and distorts our view of the future.

Accepting a child's dictation is the equivalent of robbing the child of a parent.
—*Mildred Newman and Bernard Berkowitz*

Many parents are afraid of their children. Yes, *afraid*. They're afraid that their children won't approve of them, love them, or be their pals.

Some of us give in because we feel guilty. We have so little time to spend with our children that we want all of the time to be as pleasant and conflict-free as possible. This may act in our immediate best interests, but the price we pay is having children who rule the roost.

All of us want to be loved by our children. But at what cost? If we accept the dictates of our children, whom are we helping? Children really want direction, attention, and the genuine interest that is implied by parents who are not afraid to lead.

◆

I'm told to allow my children to voice their wants, their opinions, their needs. Yes, I want them to be open to me, but I need to remember I am their leader and that they look to me for guidance.

I worry about people who get born nowadays because they get born into such tiny families—sometimes into no family at all. When you're the only pea in the pod, your parents are likely to get you confused with the Hope Diamond.

—*Russell Baker*

We know about "overparenting," about giving our child so much attention that we may seem to be studying and serving an alien. And that's just what we get if we keep up the nonstop attention—an alien.

Yes, each of our children is precious—far more precious than the Hope Diamond. But when we are overboard in our parenting, we give our child a self-image that is overinflated and grossly inappropriate.

These overparented children grow up believing that they are extraordinary—and impervious to the confines of adult life. What a terrible thing to do! We need to introduce our children not just to their own realities, but also to the realities of life. If we crowned them, they will be shocked to learn that they have no dominion to rule.

◆

I need to beware of my own best intentions. I may create a child who thinks she's the heir to the riches of the world.

It's the three pairs of eyes that mothers have to have...one pair that sees through closed doors...another in the back of her head...and, of course, the ones in front that can look at a child when he goofs up and reflect "I understand and I love you" without so much as uttering a word.

—*Erma Bombeck*

We all know that look. It is the face that needs no voice. The message gets across and is felt forever.

To really love your child is often to say nothing at all. Anyone can say "I love you." It takes a voice deep in our hearts to convey the empathy, the connectedness, the dedication of self that only a parent—mother or father—can give.

Adult lovers may have something that approximates this form of sacred communication, but there is a special, unique way in which the eyes of the parent meet the eyes of the child that says, "You are loved, unconditionally, totally."

◆

No words can really convey the deep love I have for my children. I know that there are moments of stress and strain that do not necessarily prompt words but rather action, reaction, quiet appreciation, a look of love.

BIBLIOGRAPHY

Andrews, Robert. *The Concise Columbia Dictionary of Quotations*. Avon Books, 1989.

Augarde, A.J. *The Oxford Dictionary of Modern Quotations*. Oxford University Press, 1991.

Baker, Daniel B. *Power Quotes*. Visible Ink Press, 1992.

Bartlett, John. *Bartlett's Familiar Quotations*. Little, Brown, 15th ed., 1980.

Beattie, Melody. *Beyond Codependency: And Getting Better All the Time*. Harper/Hazelden, 1987.

Beattie, Melody. *Codependent No More*. Harper/Hazelden, 1986.

Beattie, Melody. *The Language of Letting Go*. Harper/Hazelden, 1990.

Bloomfield, Harold H., M.D. *Making Peace with Your Parents*. Random House, 1983.

Bolander, Donald O., et al. *Instant Quotation Dictionary*. Career Pub., 1989.

Byrne, Robert. *The Third & Possibly the Best Six Hundred & Thirty-Seven Things Anybody Ever Said*. Fawcett, 1986.

Byrne, Robert. *One Thousand Nine Hundred Eleven Best Things Anybody Ever Said*. Fawcett Columbine, 1988.

Camp, Wesley D. *What a Piece of Work Is Man! Camp's Unfamiliar Quotations from 2000 B.C. to the Present*. Prentice Hall, 1990.

Carola, Leslie. *Motherhood*. Longmeadow Press, 1992.

Cosgrove, Melba, Harold Bloomfield, and Peter McWilliams. *How to Survive the Loss of a Love*. Bantam Books, 1976, 1991.

Donadio, Stephen, Joan Smith, Susan Mesner, and Rebecca

Davison. *The New York Public Library Book of 20th Century Quotations*. Warner Books, 1992.

Fassel, Diane. *Working Ourselves to Death*. HarperSan Francisco, 1990.

Fitzhenry, Robert I. (ed.). *Barnes & Noble Book of Quotations*. Harper, 1987.

Gardner, John W., and Francesca Gardner Reese (eds.). *Quotations of Wit and Wisdom*. W. W. Norton & Company, 1975.

Griffith, Joe. *Speakers Library of Business*. Prentice Hall, 1990.

Gross, John (ed.). *The Oxford Book of Aphorisms*. Oxford, 1992.

Henry, Lewis C. *The Best Quotations for All Occasions*. Fawcett, 1990.

Kaufman, Barry Neil. *Happiness Is a Choice*. Fawcett, 1991.

Klein, Allen. *Quotations to Cheer You Up When the World Is Getting You Down*. Sterling Publishing, 1982.

Lieberman, Gerald F. *Three Thousand Five Hundred Good Quotes for Speakers*. Doubleday, 1983.

Mackay, Harvey. *Beware the Naked Man Who Offers You His Shirt*. William Morrow, 1990.

Malloy, Merrit, and Shauna Sorensen (eds.). *The Quotable Quote Book*. Citadel Press, 1990.

Murphy, Edward F. *Two Thousand Seven Hundred & Fifteen One Line Quotations for Speakers, Writers & Raconteurs*. Crown, 1981.

Otis, Harry B. (ed.). *Simple Truths: The Best of the Cockle Bur*. Andrews & McMeel, 1990.

Park, Clara Claiborne. *The Siege*. Little, Brown, 1982.

Running Press Staff (ed.). The Quotable Woman. Running Press, 1991.

Rees, Nigel. *The Phrase That Launched 1000 Ships*. Dell, 1991.

Rosellini, Gayle, and Mark Worden. *Strong Choices, Weak Choices: The Challenge of Change in Recovery* Harper/ Hazelden, 1988.

Safire, William, and Leonard Safir. *Words of Wisdom*. Simon & Schuster/Fireside, 1989.

Saltzman, Amy. *Down-Shifting*. HarperCollins, 1991.

Schaef, Anne Wilson. *Escape from Intimacy*. HarperSan Francisco, 1989.

Schaef, Anne Wilson, and Diane Fassel. *The Addictive Organization*. Harper and Row, 1985.

Seldes, George. *The Great Quotations*. Citadel Press, 1990.

Simpson, James (compiled by). *Simpson's Contemporary Quotations*. Houghton Mifflin, 1988.

Sweeting, George. *Great Quotes & Illustrations*. Word Books, 1985.

Thomsett, Michael C. *A Treasury of Business Quotations*. Ballantine Books, 1990.

Tuttle Dictionary of Quotations for Speeches. Charles E. Tuttle Company, 1992.

Warner, Carolyn. *The Last Word: A Treasury of Women's Quotes*. Prentice Hall, 1992.

Winokur, Jon. *Friendly Advice*. Penguin/Plume, 1992.

Winokur, Jon (ed.). *True Confessions*. Dutton, 1992.

Winokur, Jon. *Zen to Go*. NAL Books, 1989.

INDEX